REFERENCE

D1095533

DOES NOT CIRCULATE

The Book of American
Trade Marks/9
The Annual of Trade Mark Design

David E. Carter

Book Design
Stephanie Fulton

First Printing, 1984

No design in this book may be copied
without the permission of the owner
of the mark.

ART DIRECTION BOOK COMPANY
10 East 39th Street
New York, NY 10016

(212) 889-6500

Library of Congress Catalog Card Number: 72-76493
International Standard Book Number: 0-88108-020-9
ISBN for Standing Orders for this series: 0910158-38-X

How to submit marks for future volumes.

This book is part of a series which shows good examples of contemporary design of trade marks, corporate symbols and logos.

Designers are invited to submit marks for possible inclusion in future volumes. Work submitted must adhere to the following guidelines:

(1) marks must be sent in the actual size they are to be reproduced in the book. Any marks not meeting this standard will be eliminated from consideration.

(2) do not mount the work.

(3) include the name of the client, and the one name to appear in the credit line as designer.

(4) send a letter giving permission for the marks to be included in the book.

Due to the large amount of material received each year, it is impossible for us to acknowledge receipt of marks.

All material should be sent to: David E. Carter, Trade Marks, P.O. Box 591, Ashland, Kentucky 41105.

8359

8363

8360

8364

8361

8365

8362

8366

8367

8368

8369

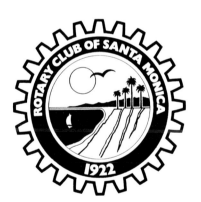

8359 American Home Energy
Designer: Spyros Dellaportas

8360 Review Films Inc.
Designer: Spyros Dellaportas

8361 Stevco, Inc.
Designer: Spyros Dellaportas

8362 Copan, Inc.
Designer: Spyros Dellaportas

8363 Park Place
Designer: Spyros Dellaportas

8364 Napoc, Inc.
Designer: Spyros Dellaportas

8365 Parnas Corp.
Designer: Spyros Dellaportas

8366 Napoc, Inc.
Designer: Spyros Dellaportas

8367 Professional Artist Management
Designer: Spyros Dellaportas

8368 Shield Insurance
Designer: Spyros Dellaportas

8369 Rotary Club of Santa Monica
Designer: Spyros Dellaportas

8370 Mourka, Inc.
Designer: Spyros Dellaportas

8370

8371

8375

8372

8376

8373

8377

8374

8378

8379

The Diplomat

8380

Furopean American Sales Union

FOR JEWELRY, WATCHES AND PRECIOUS STONES

8381

AQUA-O CORPORATION

8382

BABTON Lighting Center

8383

8387

8384

8388

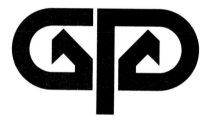

8385

8389

8386

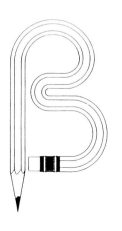

8390

8391

8392

8393

8394

8383   Santa Monica Cultural Arts
       Committee
       Designer: Spyros Dellaportas

8384   Napoc. Inc.
       Designer: Spyros Dellaportas

8385   Copan, Inc.
       Designer: Spyros Dellaportas

8386   Ben Bronson
       Designer: Spyros Dellaportas

8387   Panco, Inc.
       Designer: Spyros Dellaportas

8388   George Polycrated & Assoc.
       Designer: Spyros Dellaportas

8389   Napoc, Inc.
       Designer: Spyros Dellaportas

8390   E.A.S.T.
       Designer: Spyros Dellaportas

8391   Spyros Dellaportas
       Designer: Spyros Dellaportas

8392   Barton National
       Designer: Spyros Dellaportas

8393   Copan, Inc.
       Designer: Spyros Dellaportas

8394   Meridian Corporation
       Designer: Spyros Dellaportas

8395

8399

8396

8400

8397

8401

8398

8402

8403

8404

8405

8395   Terra Resources
       Designer: Lonnie Whittington

8396   Pat Darum
       Designer: Lonnie Whittington

8397   Associated Lithographers
       Designer: Lonnie Whittington

8398   Sigma Group
       Designer: Lonnie Whittington

8399   Everest '85
       Designer: Jean Wong

8400   Applied Micro Solutions
       Designer: Al Luna

8401   Mastercraft Plastics
       Designer: Al Luna

8402   Mikasa
       Designer: Lonnie Whittington
       & Al Luna

8403   Arizona Lobster & Seafood Co.
       Designer: Jean Wong

8404   Air Scottsdale
       Designer: Lonnie Whittington
       & Al Luna

8405   Western Education Inc.
       Designer: Al Luna

8406   Metalogic
       Designer: Lonnie Whittington
       & Al Luna

8406

8407

8411

8408

8412

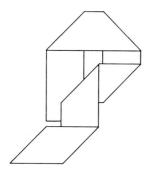

8409

8413

8410

8414

8415

Cash Sullivan &Cross

8416

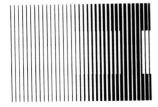

8417

8418

8419

8423

CORTEZ
CORP

8420

8424

DATA
BASE

8421

Kaibab

8425

8422

8426

DSA

8427

Mikasa

8428

brene

8429

8430

8431

8435

8432

8436

8433

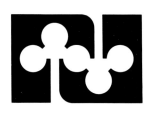

8437

8434

8438

8439

8440

8441

8442

8431   Rhythm Aerobics Studio
       Designer: Jean Wong

8432   Etienne's French Restaurant
       Designer: Jean Wong

8433   The Mews on Tenth Place
       Designer: Jean Wong

8434   Pictures
       Designer: Jean Wong

8435   Greenbrier Shopping Mall
       Designer: Emil M. Cohen

8436   Twelve Oaks Shopping Mall
       Designer: Emil M. Cohen

8437   NewPark Shopping Mall
       Designer: Emil M. Cohen

8438   Centennial Valley Shopping Mall
       Designer: Emil M. Cohen

8439   The Hennesey Construction Co.
       Designer: Emil M. Cohen

8440   Burnsville Center Shopping Mall
       Designer: Emil M. Cohen

8441   Foxboro Shopping Mall
       Designer: Emil M. Cohen

8442   Spring Hill Shopping Mall
       Designer: Emil M. Cohen

8443

8447

8444

8448

8445

8449

8446

8450

8451

8452

8453

8454

8443   Louis Joliet Shopping Mall
Designer: Emil M. Cohen

8444   Deerbrook Shopping Mall
Designer: Emil M. Cohen

8445   Willowbrook Shopping Mall
Designer: Emil M. Cohen

8446   Meadowbrook Shopping Mall
Designer: Emil M. Cohen

8447   Pinebrook Shopping Mall
Designer: Emil M. Cohen

8448   Baybrook Shopping Mall
Designer: Emil M. Cohen

8449   Westgate Shopping Mall
Designer: Emil M. Cohen

8450   Richland Fashion Mall
Designer: Emil M. Cohen

8451   The Evanston Symphony Orchestra
Designer: Emil M. Cohen

8452   School Spirit
Designer: Emil M. Cohen

8453   The Allen Woods Co.
Designer: Emil M. Cohen

8454   Keogh Motivation Plans, Inc.
Designer: Emil M. Cohen

8455

8459

Northfield
Township
Arts Council

8456

8460

8457

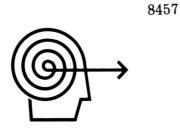

8461

8458

8462

8463

8464

8465

8455	Music for the Children of Israel Designer: Emil M. Cohen
8456	Am Sholom Congregation Designer: Emil M. Cohen
8457	Communications Research, Inc. Designer: Emil M. Cohen
8458	The Ram Engineering Co. Designer: Emil M. Cohen
8459	Northfield Township Arts Council Designer: Emil M. Cohen
8460	LaSalle Planning Co. Designer: Emil M. Cohen
8461	The Rock Island Railroad Designer: Emil M. Cohen
8462	The Colt Construction Co. Designer: Emil M. Cohen
8463	Emil M. Cohen Designer: Emil M. Cohen
8464	Friends of the Wilmette Public Library Designer: Emil M. Cohen
8465	The Chicago Commoisseur Designer: Emil M. Cohen

8466

8470

8467

8471

8468

BEECH·NUT ®

8472

8469

8473

Starburst ®

8474

8475

8476

8466	La Choy Food Products Designer: Dixon & Parcels Assoc.
8467	Scott Paper Company Designer: Dixon & Parcels Assoc.
8468	Beech-Nut Foods Corp. Designer: Dixon & Parcels Assoc.
8469	Harbor Sweets Ltd. Designer: Dixon & Parcels Assoc.
8470	M&M/Mars Snack Master Div. Designer: Dixon & Parcels Assoc.
8471	R.M. Palmer Company Designer: Dixon & Parcels Assoc.
8472	Gougeon Brothers Inc. Designer: Dixon & Parcels Assoc.
8473	M&M/Mars , Inc. Snack Master Div. Designer: Dixon & Parcels Assoc.
8474	Austin Foods Company Designer: Dixon & Parcels Assoc.
8475	National Industries for the Blind Designer: Dixon & Parcels Assoc.
8476	Georgia Southern College Designer: Dixon & Parcels Assoc.

8477

8481

8478

8482

Luminall.

8479

8483

Combos™

8480

PATiO

8484

8485

8486

8487

8488

8477   Krispy Kreme Doughnut Corp.
Designer: Dixon & Parcels Assoc.

8478   Bernan Foods Inc.
Designer: Dixon & Parcels Assoc.

8479   Superior Pet Products Inc.
Designer: Dixon & Parcels Assoc.

8480   Del Monte
Designer: Dixon & Parcels Assoc.

8481   National Sea Products
Designer: Dixon & Parcels Assoc.

8482   Luminall Paints Inc.
Designer: Dixon & Parcels Assoc.

8483   M&M/Mars Snack Master Div.
Designer: Dixon & Parcels Assoc.

8484   ITT Continental Banking Company
Designer: Dixon & Parcels Assoc.

8485   The Pennsylvania State University
Designer: Dixon & Parcels Assoc.

8486   Cadillac Pet Foods, Inc.
Designer: Dixon & Parcels Assoc.

8487   Maripac International
Designer: Dixon & Parcels Assoc.

8488   Young Drug Products Corp.
Designer: Dixon & Parcels Assoc.

8489

8493

8490

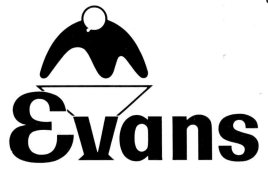

8491

8494

8492

8495

8496

8497

8498

8489	Wilber Chocolate Co., Inc. Designer: Dixon & Parcels Assoc.
8490	E.B. Evans Inc. Designer: Dixon & Parcels Assoc.
8491	Superior Pet Products Inc. Designer: Dixon & Parcels Assoc.
8492	ITT Continental Banking Company Designer: Dixon & Parcels Assoc.
8493	Pennsylvania Dutch-Megs Inc. Designer: Dixon & Parcels Assoc.
8494	Borden Inc. Designer: Dixon & Parcels Assoc.
8495	Crest Eastern Corp. Designer: Dixon & Parcels Assoc.
8496	Industrial Valley Bank Designer: Dixon & Parcels Assoc.
8497	The Bachman Company Designer: Dixon & Parcels Assoc.
8498	Dari Farms Designer: Dixon & Parcels Assoc.

8499

BANK
OF MID-JERSEY

8502

8500

PFEIFFER

8503

BONOMO

8501

8504

8505

Action Philadelphia

8506

8507

8499	Bank of Mid-Jersey Designer: Dixon & Parcels Assoc.
8500	Pfeiffer's Foods, Inc. Designer: Dixon & Parcels Assoc.
8501	Bonomo Candy Company Designer: Dixon & Parcels Assoc.
8502	4C Foods Corp. Designer: Dixon & Parcels Assoc.
8503	Gold Medal Candy Corp. Designer: Dixon & Parcels Assoc.
8504	Youngs Drug Products Corp. Designer: Dixon & Parcels Assoc.
8505	Action Philadelphia Designer: Dixon & Parcels Assoc.
8506	Franklin Papers Designer: Douglas Wilson
8507	Paradise Found Designer: Douglas Wilson

The Lincoln Theater

8508

8512

ARI **ACCOUNTING RESOURCES INTERNATIONAL**

8509

the **FOLKS** at **COMPANY**

8513

dexter
DATA SYSTEMS INC.

8510

8514

Twin Anchors Marina

8511

8515

Rochester Steel

8516

8517

8518

Family Counseling Center

8519

Catholic Charity Committee

8520

8524

jazz band

8521

8525

Weber Management Dynamics

8522

8526

AMERICA'S FINEST!

8523

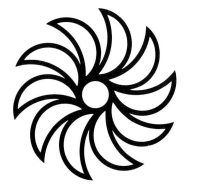

8527

Southwind

8528

8529

8530

8531

8520 Gordon Reese
      Designer: Douglas Wilson

8521 Spencer Group
      Designer: Douglas Wilson

8522 The Boats Sail Inn
      Designer: Douglas Wilson

8523 Sun Ray Products, Inc.
      Designer: Douglas Wilson

8524 Dixie 5
      Designer: Douglas Wilson

8525 Weber Management
      Designer: Douglas Wilson

8526 Th Cleaners
      Designer: Doug Granger

8527 Southwind Ultralights, Inc.
      Designer: Doug Granger

8528 Media National Corporation
      Designer: Doug Granger

8529 Genesis Network
      Designer: Doug Granger

8530 Genesis Production Corporation
      Designer: Doug Granger

8531 Genesis Management Corporation
      Designer: Doug Granger

8532

8536

8533

8537

8534

8538

8535

MIRRIM

8539

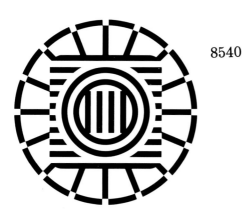

8540

8541

8542

VIDATEL

8543

8532 Omnimark, Ltd.
Designer: Doug Granger

8533 Geovest, Ltd.
Designer: Doug Granger

8534 Continuum, Ltd.
Designer: Doug Granger

8535 Mirrim
Designer: Doug Granger

8536 Shaw Resources
Designer: Doug Granger

8537 Dynagraphics, Inc.
Designer: Doug Granger

8538 Family Dental, PA
Designer: Doug Granger

8539 Lyman Oil Company
Designer: Doug Granger

8540 Vidatel
Designer: Doug Granger

8541 Papillon
Designer: Doug Granger

8542 Westmoreland, McGarity & Pitts
Designer: Doug Granger

8543 LGM, Inc.
Designer: Doug Granger

8544

8548

KRISTA'MI

8545

8549

8546

8550

8551

8547

8552

8553

Women in Free Enterprise

8554

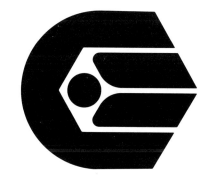

8555

8544 Metropolitan Arts Council
      Designer: Doug Granger

8545 Carolina Computer Stores
      Designer: Doug Granger

8546 Creative International, Inc.
      Designer: Doug Granger

8547 Sundowners, Inc.
      Designer: Jim Adams

8548 Kristami
      Designer: Jim Adams

8549 Volunteer State Corporate Central
      Credit Union
      Designer: Jim Adams

8550 moi, inc.
      Designer: Jim Adams

8551 Steve Chambers Architects
      Designer: Jim Adams

8552 Sherman Research Corporation
      Designer: Jim Adams

8553 McMurray Foundation
      Designer: Jim Adams

8554 Cameron Manufacturing Co.
      Designer: Jim Adams

8555 Four Star Oil & Gas
      Designer: Jim Adams

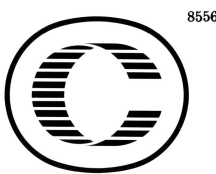

8556

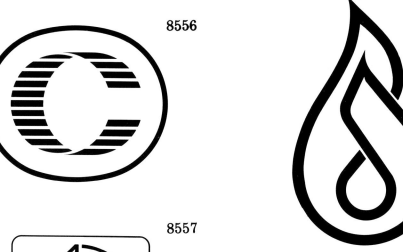

8560

8557

GRANT/
THOMPSON

8561

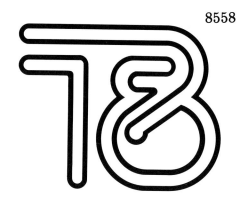

8558

8562

8563

8559

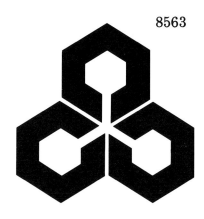

8564

8565

8566

8556	Christopher National Press	Designer: Jim Adams
8557	Grant/Thompson	Designer: Jim Adams
8558	T & B Scottdale Contractors	Designer: Don Connelly
8559	Electromagnetic Systems Inc.	Designer: Don Connelly
8560	Professional Association Management	Designer: Don Connelly
8561	Alvin Lee Construction	Designer: Don Connelly
8562	Shaw & Parrott Racing	Designer: Don Connelly
8563	College Coaches Classic	Designer: Don Connelly
8564	Automated Marketing	Designer: Don Connelly
8565	Condor Automotive Services	Designer: Don Connelly
8566	Newspaper in Education	Designer: Don Connelly
8567	The Selin Company	Designer: Don Connelly

8567

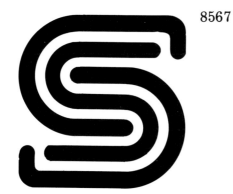

8568

8572

8569

8573

8574

8570

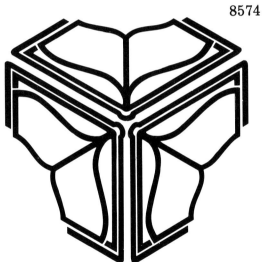

8571

8575

8576

8577

8578

8579

8568   Georgia Special Olympics
        Designer: Don Connelly

8569   Cotton States Classic
        (proposal)
        Designer: Don Connelly

8570   Real Property Law Section
        Designer: Don Connelly

8571   Metro Amateur Golf
        Designer: Don Connelly

8572   Hampton Green
        Designer: Don Connelly

8573   Hampton Oaks
        Designer: Don Connelly

8574   Commission on Continuing Lawyer
        Competency
        Designer: Don Connelly

8575   Girafix Grafix
        Designer: Don Connelly

8576   Trans-America
        Designer: Don Connelly

8577   Sun Dynasty
        Designer: Don Connelly

8578   Avondale Community Action
        Designer: Con Connelly

8579   Park Place South
        Designer: Don Connelly

8580

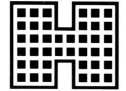

8581

8582

Cincinnati
Zoo

8583

Cincinnati
Zoo

8584

8585

8586

8587

AGC

8588

8589

8590

8591

8580   HOBIS
       Designer: Don Connelly

8581   Big Heart Award
       Designer: Don Connelly

8582   Cincinnati Zoo
           (proposal)
       Designer: Robert Probst

8583   Cincinnati Zoo
           (proposal)
       Designer: Robert Probst

8584   Cincinnati Zoo
           (proposal)
       Designer: Robert Probst

8585   Cincinnati Zoo
           (proposal)
       Designer: Robert Probst

8586   Cincinnati Zoo
           (proposal)
       Designer: Robert Probst

8587   American General Communications
       Designer: Max A. McDonald

8588   Home Product Installers
       Designer: Max A. McDonald

8589   Max McDonald Design Office
       Designer: Max A. McDonald

8590   Tom Thornburg, Painter
       Designer: Max A. McDonald

8591   Tom's Paint Store
       Designer: Max A. McDonald

8592

8596

8593

8597

8594

8598

8595

8599

8600

Westfield
by-the-railroad

8601

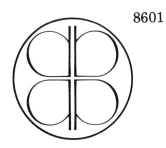

8602

8603

8592   Central Home Health Care
        Designer: Max A. McDonald

8593   Sea-Temp Instrument Company
        Designer: Max A. McDonald

8594   Formakers
        Designer: Max A. McDonald

8595   Marglotex
        Designer: Max A. McDonald

8596   Decal Advertising
        Designer: Max A. McDonald

8597   Insights West
        Designer: Max A. McDonald

8598   KTRE-TV 9
        Designer: Debbie Brumfield

8599   Venture Construction Co.
        Designer: Debbie Brumfield

8600   Westfield
        Designer: Debbie Brumfield

8601   Debbie Brumfield Design
        Designer: Debbie Brumfield

8602   Christian Information & Service
            Center
        Designer: Debbie Brumfield

8603   Hardwood Designs
        Designer: Debbie Brumfield

8604

8608

8605

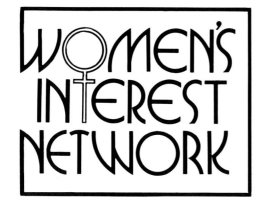

8609

TIMBERLINE
HOMES

8606

8610

8607

8611

8612

8613

8604 Wenger- Brumfield Advertising
Designer: Debbie Brumfield

8605 Women's Interest Network
Designer: Debbie Brumfield

8606 Images Audio-Visual Services
Designer: The Malone Group

8607 Palm Beach Cafe
Designer: The Malone Group

8608 City Center Discoteque
Designer: The Malone Group

8609 Timberline Homes
Designer: The Malone Group

8610 Restaurant Chain
Designer: The Malone Group

8611 Heartland Record Co.
Designer: The Malone Group

8612 Gourmet Restaurant
Designer: The Malone Group

8613 Ponte Vedra Square
Designer: The Malone Group

8614 Bimini Bay Development
Designer: The Malone Group

8615 Calvary Ministries International
Designer: The Malone Group

8614

8615

8616

TRECO

8617

NORRIS

8618

ORTEGA·RIVERFRONT·HOMES

PIRATES BAY

8619

HAYES
STREET
CARRIAGE
HOUSE

8620

8621

8622

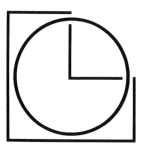

8623

8624

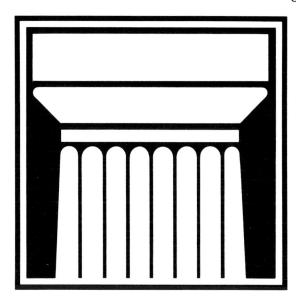

8625

8626

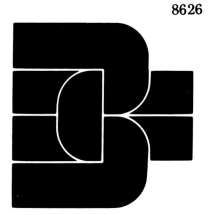

8630

SHAPIRO
MELLINGER

8627

8631

8628

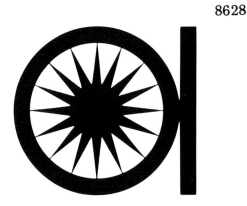

8632

8629

G⬤⬤ING PLACES

8633

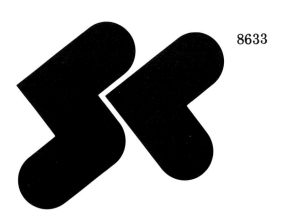

8634

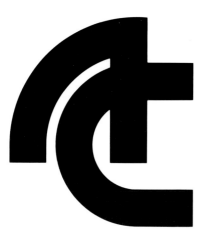

8635

8636

8637

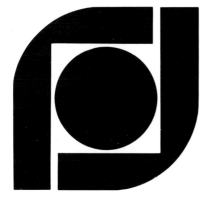

8638

8641

8639

8642

8640

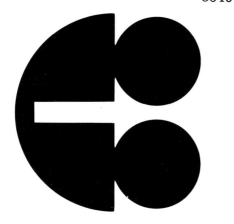

8643

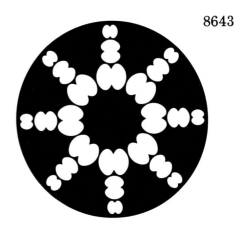

8644

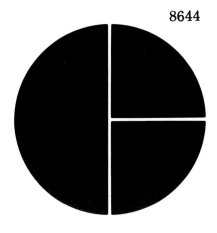

8645

8646

8638   Ellerman Companies, Inc.
Designer: Jim Lienhart

8639   Management Organization Inc.
Designer: Jim Lienhart

8640   General Sintering Corporation
Designer: Jim Lienhart

8641   Sphere
Designer: Jim Lienhart

8642   Savings & Loan News
Designer: Jim Lienhart

8643   Diamond International, Inc.
Designer: Jim Lienhart

8644   Chicago Graphics, Inc.
Designer: Jim Lienhart

8645   Tero Corvette
Designer: Jim Lienhart

8646   Color Communications, Inc.
Designer: Jim Lienhart

8647

8650

8648

8651

8649

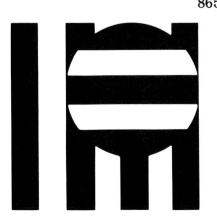

8652

8653

8654

8655

8656

ultimo

8659

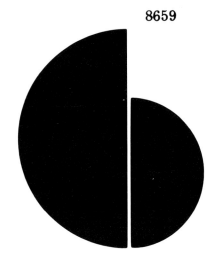

8657

8660

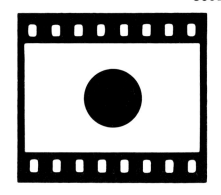

8858

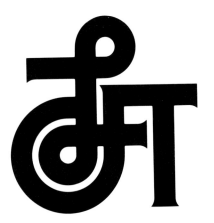

8661

8662

DAN M●RRILL

8663

8664

WHITTLE RADDON MOTLEY & HANKS

8665

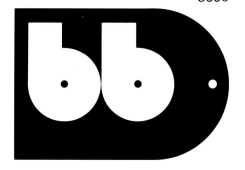

8666

8669

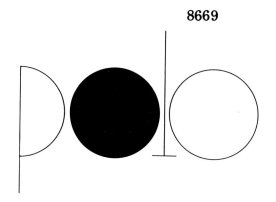

8667

8670

8668

8671

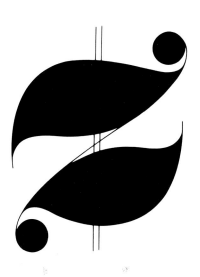

8672

8673

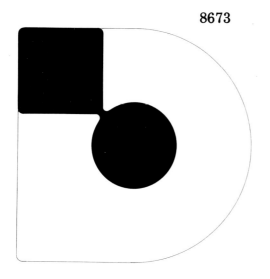

8674

8675

von

8678

8676

8679

it

8677

curtiss

8680

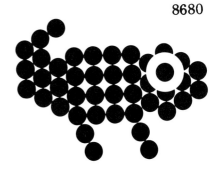

8681

8682

8675 Von Photography
      Designer: Jim Lienhart

8676 W. Clement Stone
      Designer: Jim Lienhart

8677 Curtiss, Inc,
      Designer: Jim Lienhart

8678 Stockyard Inn
      Designer: Jim Lienhart

8679 International Typetronics
      Designer: Jim Lienhart

8680 Chameleon Color Crafts
      Designer: Jim Lienhart

8681 Reflections of You
      Designer: Jim Lienhart

8682 Congregational Church of Glen Ellyn
      Designer: Jim Lienhart

8683 Mutual Employment Inc.
      Designer: Jim Lienhart

8683

8684

8687

8685

SAVINGS & LOAN NEWS

8688

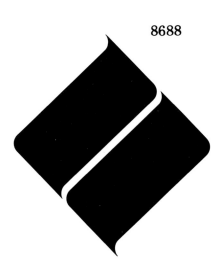

8686

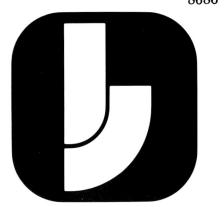

8689

8690

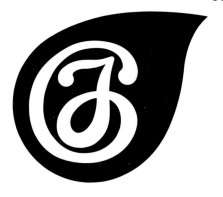

8691

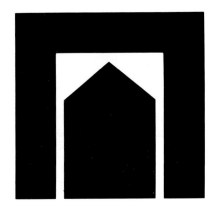

8692

8684   Cityhouse
        Designer: Jim Lienhart

8685   Savings & Loan News
        Designer: Jim Lienhart

8686   Bank Administration Institute
        Designer: Jim Lienhart

8687   Pacesetter Bank
        Designer: Jim Lienhart

8688   Institute of Financial Education/
        U.S. Saving League
        Designer: Jim Lienhart

8689   College of Du Page
        Designer: Jim Lienhart

8690   Jean Grow
        Designer: Jim Lienhart

8691   Beliard Gordon and Associates
        Designer: Jim Lienhart

8692   Gary National Bank
        Designer: Jim Lienhart

8693

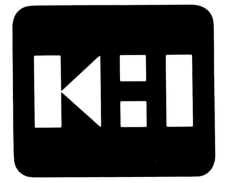

8696

8694

8697

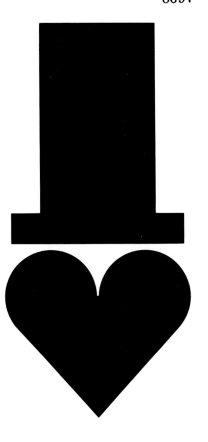

8695

8698

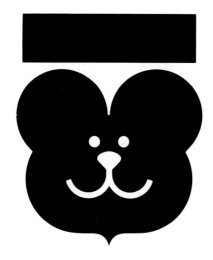

8699

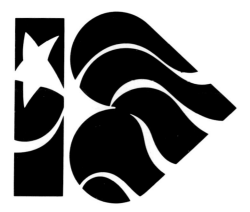

8700

8693   Kollar Heinz, Inc.
       Designer: Jim Lienhart

8694   Photronic Typographers, Inc.
       Designer: Jim Lienhart

8695   Savings Institutions
       Designer: Jim Lienhart

8696   Series of Promotional Trademarks
          for Jim Lienhart
       Designer: Jim Lienhart

8697   Jim Lienhart
          (He's Honest)
       Designer: Jim Lienhart

8698   Jim Lienhart
          (He's Cuddly)
       Designer: Jim Lienhart

8699   Jim Lienhart
          (He's Patriotic)
       Designer: Jim Lienhart

8700   Jim Lienhart
          (He's Romantic)
       Designer: Jim Lienhart

8701

8702

8703

8704

8705

8706

8707

8708

8701   Jim Lienhart
        (He's Debonair)
        Designer: Jim Lienhart

8702   Jim Lienhart
        (He's Emotional)
        Designer: Jim Lienhart

8703   Jim Lienhart
        (He's Athletic)
        Designer: Jim Lienhart

8704   Jim Lienhart
        (He's Creative)
        Designer: Jim Lienhart

8705   Jim Lienhart
        (He's Diligent)
        Designer: Jim Lienhart

8706   Hider Energy System, Inc.
        Designer: Lesniewicz/Navarre

8707   Libbey-Owens-Ford Co.
        Designer: Lesniewicz/Navarre

8708   Bailey
        Designer: Lesniewicz/Navarre

8709   SBS/Construction Management, Inc.
        Designer: Lesniewicz/ Navarre

8709

8710

RPOD

8714

8711

8715

8712

8716

8713

8717

8718

8719

8720

8721

8710 Owens-Corning Fiberglas
Corporation
Designer: Lesniewicz/Navarre

8711 Owens-Corning Fiberglas
Corporation
Designer: Lesniewicz/Navarre

8712 Owens-Corning Fiberglas
Corporation
Designer: Lesniewicz/Navarre

8713 Owens-Corning Fiberglas
Corporation
Designer: Lesniewicz/Navarre

8714 Owens-Corning Fiberglas
Corporation
Designer: Lesniewicz/Navarre

8715 Owens-Corning Fiberglas
Corporation
Designer: Lesniewicz/Navarre

8716 Owens-Corning Fiberglas
Corporation
Designer: Lesniewicz/Navarre

8717 Owens-Corning Fiberglas
Corporation
Designer: Lesniewicz/Navarre

8718 Owens-Corning Fiberglas
Corporation
Designer: Lesniewicz/Navarre

8719 Owens-Corning Fiberglas
Corporation
Designer: Lesniewicz/ Navarre

8720 Owens-Corning Fiberglas
Corporation
Designer: Lesniewicz/Navarre

8721 Owens-Corning Fiberglas
Corporation
Designer: Lesniewicz/Navarre

8722

8726

8723

8727

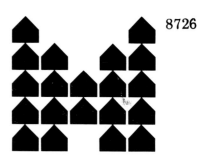

8724

8728

8725

8729

8730

8731

8732

8733

8722	Owens-Illinois	Designer: Lesniewicz/Navarre
8723	Owens-Illinois	Designer: Lesniewicz/Navarre
8724	Owens-Illinois	Designer: Lesniewicz/Navarre
8725	Ritter	Designer: Lesniewicz/Navarre
8726	Mohon Realty	Designer: Lesniewicz/Navarre
8727	Mohon Realty	Designer: Lesniewicz/Navarre
8728	Mohon Realty	Designer: Lesniewicz/Navarre
8729	Bostleman Corporation	Designer: Lesniewicz/Navarre
8730	Dana/Spicer/Chelsea	Designer: Lesniewicz/Navarre
8731	Dana/Spicer/Chelsea	Designer: Lesniewicz/Navarre
8732	Dana/Spicer/Chelsea	Designer: Lesniewicz/Navarre
8733	Dana/Spicer/Chelsea	Designer: Lesniewicz/Navarre

8734

8738

8735

8739

8736

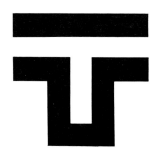

8740

8737

8741

8742

8743

8744

8745

8734   Vetus
       Designer: Lesniewicz/Navarre

8735   Ursula Cauffiel School of Music
       Designer: Lesniewicz/Navarre

8736   Tuschman Steel
       Designer: Lesniewicz/Navarre

8737   The Toledo Museum of Art
       Designer: Lesniewicz/Navarre

8738   Dunbar Mechanical
       Designer: Lesniewicz/Navarre

8739   Gary Lesniewicz
       Designer: Lesniewicz/Navarre

8740   Personal Touch
       Designer: Lesniewicz/Navarre

8741   Elan Energy
       Designer: Lesniewicz/Navarre

8742   Westbrook
       Designer: Lesniewicz/Navarre

8743   Camp Hemlock
       Designer: Lesniewicz/Navarre

8744   Gordon Grant
       Designer: Lesniewicz/Navarre

8745   Professionel, Inc.
       Designer: Lesniewicz/Navarre

8746

8750

8747

8751

8748

8752

8749

8753

8754

8755

8756

8757

8746   Jim Yark
       Designer: Lesniewicz/Navarre

8747   Professional Planning Services
       Designer: Lesniewicz/Navarre

8748   Country Equine
       Designer: Lesniewicz/Navarre

8749   Finks Fine Foods
       Designer: Lesniewicz/Navarre

8750   Jeff Fout Stables
       Designer: Lesniewicz/Navarre

8751   St. Lukes Hospital
       Designer: Lesniewicz/Navarre

8752   Toledo Popcorn Co.
       Designer: Lesniewicz/Navarre

8753   The Healthy Woman
       Designer: Lesniewicz/Navarre

8754   The French Bakery
       Designer: Lesniewicz/Navarre

8755   Jones & Henry
       Designer: Lesniewicz/Navarre

8756   Sunshine
       Designer: Lesniewicz/Navarre

8757   The Hair Depot
       Designer: Lesniewicz/Navarre

8758

Thé Hämlét

8762

8759

THE EMPORIUM
FINE FASHIONS FOR WOMEN

8763

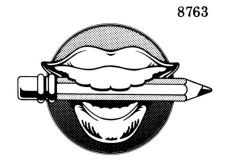

8760

PREVAIL

8764

8761

8765

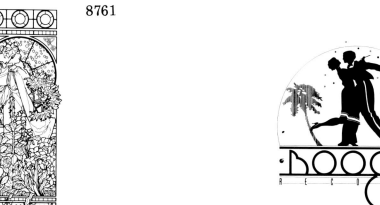

BOOGIE
RECORDS

8766

8767

8768

8769

8758	The Hamlet Designer: Lesniewicz/Navarre
8759	The Emporium Designer: Lesniewicz/Navarre
8760	Prevail Designer: Lesniewicz/Navarre
8761	Ken's Designer: Lesniewicz/Navarre
8762	Finkbeiner, Pettis & Strout, Ltd. Designer: Lesniewicz/Navarre
8763	Creatively Speaking Designer: Lesniewicz/Navarre
8764	TIVIT Designer: Lesniewicz/Navarre
8765	Boogie Records Designer: Lesniewicz/Navarre
8766	Park J. Tunes Designer: Lesniewicz/Navarre
8767	Paige One Productions Designer: Lesniewicz/Navarre
8768	ARMA Designer: Lesniewicz/Navarre
8769	Adventure Shop Designer: Lesniewicz/Navarre

8770

8774

8771

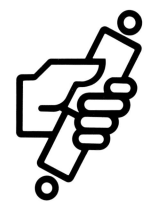

8775

8772

8776

8773

8777

8778

8779

8780

8770   Giant Products Company
       Designer: Lesniewicz/Navarre

8771   Monroe Shock
       Designer: Lesniewicz/Navarre

8772   Solar Trucking Company
       Designer: Lesniewicz/Navarre

8773   Duquette Plumbing
       Designer: Lesniewicz/Navarre

8774   Suburban Showcase of Homes
       Designer: Lesniewicz/Navarre

8775   CEMA
       Designer: Lesniewicz/Navarre

8776   Kennecorp
       Designer: Lesniewicz/Navarre

8777   Planned Parenthood
       Designer: Lesniewicz/Navarre

8778   Deopke/Lesniewicz
       Designer: Lesniewicz/Navarre

8779   WGTE
       Designer: Lesniewicz/Navarre

8780   Fantacy Hill Farms Limited
       Designer: Lesniewicz/Navarre

8781

8785

8782

8786

8783

8787

8784

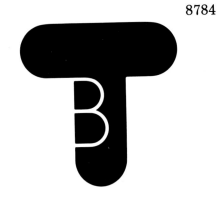

8788

8789

8790

8791

8781 The Dockside Fish Company
Designer: Kramer, Miller, Lomden, Glassman

8782 Loveladies Tennis Club
Designer: Kramer, Miller, Lomden, Glassman

8783 Tot Spot
Designer: Kramer, Miller, Lomden, Glassman

8784 Bernard Toll
Designer: Kramer, Miller, Lomden, Glassman

8785 Annenberg Cinematheque
Designer: Kramer, Miller,Lomden, Glassman

8786 1608 Walnut Street
Designer: Kramer, Miller, Lomden, Glassman

8787 Narco Scientific
Designer: Kramer, Miller, Lomden, Glassman

8788 SMS
Designer: Kramer, Miller, Lomden, Glassman

8789 Irene's Charcuterie
Designer: Kramer, Miller, Lomden. Glassman

8790 Ristorante DiLullo
Designer: Kramer, Miller, Lomden, Glassman

8791 Philadalphia Martime Museum
Designer: Kramer, Miller, Lomden, Glassman

8792

8795

8793

8796

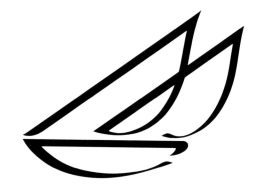

8794

8797

8798

8799

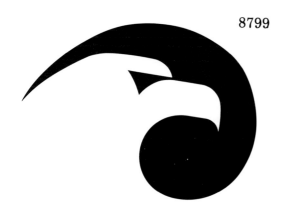

8800

8792   12 P.B.S.
Designer: Kramer, Miller, Lomden, Glassman

8793   200 P
Designer: Kramer, Miller, Lomden, Glassman

8794   Philadelphia Restaurant Festival
Designer: Kramer, Miller, Lomden, Glassman

8795   Gallery 3
Designer: Vincent J. Mielcarek

8796   Marina Cafe
Designer: Vincent J. Mielcarek

8797   Moravian Florist
Designer: Vincent J. Mielcarek

8798   Mutual Aid Project
Designer: Vincent J. Mielcarek

8799   Falcon Design, LTD
Designer: Vincent J. Mielcarek

8800   Staten Island Hospital
Designer: Vincent J. Mielcarek

8801

8803

8802

8804

8805

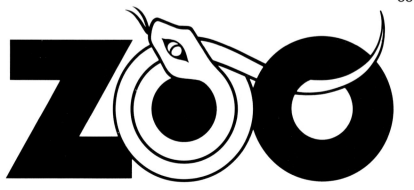

8806

8807

8808

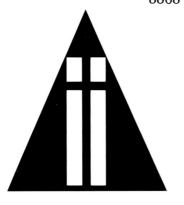

8801 Gateway State Bank
      Designer: Vincent J. Mielcarek

8802 Terra Equities
      Designer: Vincent J. Mielcarek

8803 Staten Island Botanical Garden
      Designer: Vincent J. Mielcarek

8804 College Quest
      Designer: Vincent J. Mielcarek

8805 Staten Island Zoo
      Designer: Vincent J. Mielcarek

8806 Cortina Valley
      Designer: Vincent J. Mielcarek

8807 New York City Builders Association
      Designer: Vincent J. Mielcarek

8808 Our Saviour Lutheran Church
      Designer: Vincent J. Mielcarek

8809

8811

8810

8812

8813

VALMONT TRADE CENTER

8814

COLORADO ELECTRIC

8809 Wagner College
Designer: Vincent J. Mielcarek

8810 Classroom Consortia Media
Designer: Vincent J. Mielcarek

8811 Torwest
Designer: Carole Nervig

8812 Gregg Homes Inc.
Designer: Carole Nervig

8813 Valmont Trade Center
Designer: Carole Nervig

8814 Colorado Electric
Designer: Carole Nervig

8815 Parkfield
Designer: Carole Nervig

8816 Skylink Corporation
Designer: Carole Nervig

8815

8816

8818

8819

8820

8817   Thomas C.M., Inc.
       Designer: Carole Nervig

8818   Beef & Grain Restaurant
       Designer: Neal Peterson
           Daremus & Company

8819   First National Bank & Trust
           Company
       Designer: Neal Peterson
           Daremus & Company

8820   Mary's Market
       Designer: Carl White
           Doremus & Company

8821   Communique
       Designer: Carl White
           Doremus & Company

8821

8822

Whittier Inc.

8826

SUPRACOTE

8823

CHICAGOLAND
FEDERAL SAVINGS

8827

8824

8825

superior
optical company

8828

Charles E. Hackett & Co.

8830

8831

Flagg Industries, Inc.

8822 Whittier Inc.
Designer: Carl White
        Doremus & Company

8823 Chicago Federal Savings
Designer: Carl White
        Doremus & Company

8824 The Henderson Company
Designer: Carl White
        Doremus & Company

8825 Superior Optical Company
Designer: Ray Engle & Associates

8826 Supracote
Designer: Ray Engle & Associates

8827 Photography West
Designer: Ray Engle & Associates

8828 Marcy
Designer: Ray Engle & Associates

8829 Charles E. Hackett & Co.
Designer: Ray Engle & Associates

8830 Caravelle Communities
Designer: Ray Engle & Associates

8831 Flag Industries, Inc.
Designer: Ray Engle & Associates

8832

8835

ierc

8833

8836

8834

8837

DIAMOND
PERFORATED
METALS, INC.

8838

8839

8840

8841

SEADEV INC.

8844

CALIFORNIA

8842

8845

RELIANCE

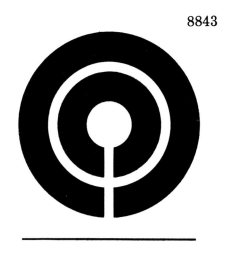

8843

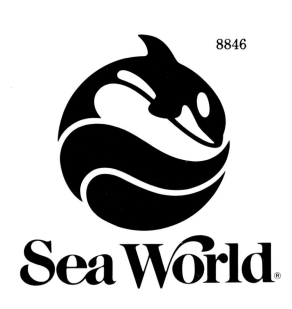

8846

Sea World®

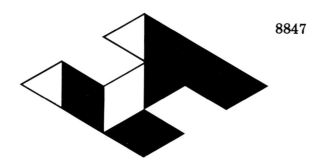

8847

HALLMARK PRODUCTIONS

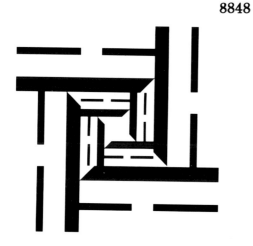

8848

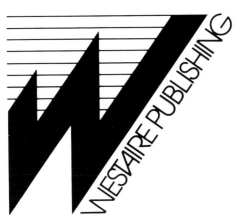

8849

8850

8853

8851

8854

8852

8855

8856

8857

8858

8859

8860

8861

PRISMATONE

8865

8862

8866

8863

8867

8864

8868

8869

8870

8861   Prismatone Paint Co.
      (hypothetical)
      Designer: Melanie Bass

8862   Unicorn Galleries
      (hypothetical)
      Designer: Melanie Bass

8863   Le Soie Boutique
      (Hypothetical)
      Designer: Melanie Bass

8864   Melanie Bass
      Designer: Melanie Bass

8865   The English Finish Advertising Co.
      Designer: Ronald R. Fichthorn

8866   J. Armistead Bray
      Designer: William L. Biles

8867   Response Technologies
      Designer: William L. Biles

8868   Ricolino
      Designer: Advance Design Center

8869   Festin Foods Corp
      Designer: Advance Design Center

8870   Marnos, S.A.
      Designer: Advance Design Center

8871   Cortina Bienes Raices
      Designer: Advance Design Center

8871

8872

8876

8877

8873

8874

8878

8875

First Capital Companies

8879

8880

8881

8882

8886

FINSBURY POINTE

T O W N H O U S E S

8883

8887

8884

8888

ASPEN·LTD

8885

8889

South Florida Group Health

8890

8891

8882   Willow Creek Condominiums
        Designer: Horwitz, Mann
            & Bukvic, Inc.

8883   Cincinnati Suburban Press, Inc.
        Designer: Horwitz, Mann
            & Bukvic, Inc.

8884   Florence Bowl
        Designer: Horwitz, Mann
            & Bukvic, Inc.

8885   Washington Federals (USFL)
        Designer: Horwitz, Mann
            & Bukvic, Inc.

8886   Finsbury Pointe Condominiums
        Designer: Horwitz, Mann
            & Bukvic, Inc.

8887   Alexander's Floral Shoppes
        Designer: Horwitz, Mann
            & Bukvic, Inc.

8888   Aspen, Ltd.
        Designer: Horwitz, Mann
            & Bukvic, Inc.

8889   South Florida Group Health
        Designer: Young & Martin Design

8890   Sandy Springs Minor Emergency
            Medical Center
        Designer: Young & Martin Design

8891   Contract Grass, Inc.
        Designer: Young & Martin Design

8892

8895

8893

AmeriHealth

8896

8894

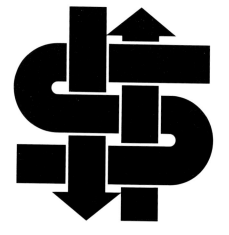

8897

Where good things develop fast.

8898

8892 R & R Evaluations, Inc.
       Designer: Young & Martin Design

8893 AmeriHealth, Inc.
       Designer: Young & Martin Design

8894 Associated Regional Accounting
         Firms
       Designer: Young & Martin Design

8895 Native Tree, Inc.
       Designer: Young & Martin Design

8896 Young & Martin Design
       Designer: Young & Martin Design

8897 Jack Rabbit Film Processing
       Designer: Harvey Dellinger

8898 Tomichi Condominiums
       Designer: Harvey Dellinger

8899 Graphics Now
       Designer: Harvey Dellinger

8900 Mountain Horizons Condominiums
       Designer: Harvey Dellinger

8899

8900

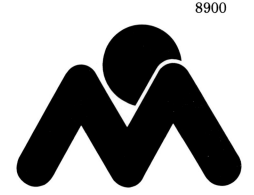

8901

8904

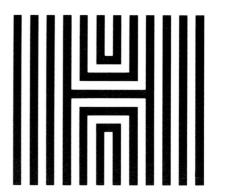

8902

8905

8903

8906

8907

8908

8909

8901 Four Oaks
Designer: Harvey Dellinger

8902 Forthill
Designer: Harvey Dellinger

8903 Structural Concepts
Designer: Paul Frick Graphic Design

8904 High Museum Gift Shop
Designer: Paul Frick Graphic Design

8905 Portables, Inc.
Designer: Paul Frick Graphic Design

8906 Venture Management, Inc.
Designer: Paul Frick Graphic Design

8907 WOWI Radio Station
Designer: Everett Forbes

8908 Colonial Institute For Child and
Adolesent Psychiatry
Designer: Everett Forbes

8909 Women's Health Forum
Designer: Everett Forbes

8910 Patrick Henry Hospital
Designer: Everett Forbes

8910

8911

8912

8913

8914

8915

8916

8917

8918

8919

8911   Worldwide Security Systems
       Designer: Constance Kovar Graphic
         Design, Inc.

8912   Atlantic Cable Television Publishing
       Designer: Constance Kovar Graphic
         Design, Inc.

8913   Ckarat Advertising
       Designer: Constance Kovar Graphic
         Design, Inc.

8914   Group Four Mail
       Designer: Constance Kovar Graphic
         Design, Inc.

8915   Ckat & Associates
       Designer: Constance Kovar Graphic
         Design, Inc.

8916   Massaro Corp Contractors
       Designer: Adam, Filippo & Moran
         Inc., Design Consultants

8917   Audio Visual Consultants
       Designer: Adam, Filippo & Moran
         Inc., Design Consultants

8918   Keystone Medical Equip. Corp Inc.
       Designer: Adam, Filippo & Moran
         Inc., Design Consultants

8919   Bar Restaurant
       Designer: Adam, Filippo & Moran
         Inc., Design Consultants

8920

300 Weyman Plaza

8924

THIRTEEN HUNDRED NEW YORK AVENUE

8921

8925

The Chef's Choice

8922

Douglas Municipal Airport
Charlotte, N.C.

8926

LAND SEA & AIR
DEVELOPMENT CORPORATION

8923

Allegheny Center

8927

Three Rivers Computer

8928

Westinghouse
Credit
Corporation

8929

8930

8920 Lucien Caste Architects
      Designer: Adam, Filippo & Moran
      Inc., Design Consultants

8921 Thompson Homes
      Designer: Adam, Filippo & Moran
      Inc., Design Consultants

8922 Douglas Municipal Airport
      Designer: Adam, Filippo & Moran
      Inc., Design Consultants

8923 Douglas Air
      Designer: Adam, Filippo & Moran
      Inc., Design Consultants

8924 DAON Corporation
      Designer: Adam, Filippo & Moran
      Inc., Design Consultants

8925 Jeaunette Glass
      Designer: Adam, Filippo & Moran
      Inc., Design Consultants

8926 Land, Sea, & Air
      Designer: Adam, Filippo & Moran
      Inc., Design Consultants

8927 Three Rivers Computer
      Designer: Adam, Filippo & Moran
      Inc., Design Consultants

8928 Westinghouse Credit Corporation
      Designer: Adam, Filippo & Moran
      Inc., Design Consultants

8929 RKS Institute
      Designer: Gina M. Palazzo

8930 Crisdel Construction Company
      Designer: Gina M. Palazzo

8931 JoAnn Palazzo, Exercise Physiologist
      Designer: Gina M. Palazzo

8931

8932

THE FIRST AGENCY

8936

Peg tight

8933

NARTA NEWS

8937

Petrini

8934

Elmwood Park Plaza

8938

8935

Foremost Corrugated
Company, Inc.

8939

Palazzo

8940

8941

8942

8932 The First Agency Insurance
      Designer: Gina M. Palazzo

8933 NARTA News
      Designer: Gina M. Palazzo

8934 Elmwood Park Plaza
      Designer: Gina M. Palazzo

8935 Foremost Corrugated Co., Inc.
      Designer: Gina M. Palazzo

8936 Pigtight
         (fictitious furniture product)
      Designer: Gina M. Palazzo

8937 Petrini Realty & Insurance Co.
      Designer: Gina M. Palazzo

8938 Robert E. Smith, Graphic Arts
      Designer: Gina M. Palazzo

8939 Palazzo Design
      Designer: Gina M. Palazzo

8940 F.H. Heating & Cooling
      Designer: Ron Matteson

8941 Scottsdale Public Schools
      Designer: Ron Matteson

8942 Minner Realty
      Designer: Ron Matteson

8943 Corporate Credit Union of Az
      Designer: Ron Matteson

8943

8944

Classic Running Boards of Arizona

8948

8945

minner realty

8949

8950

8946

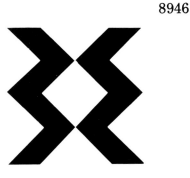

8947

MINNER

8951

professional · drivers · operators · pilots · services

employment consultants

8953

8944   Classic Running Boards of Az
        Designer: Ron Matteson

8945   Minner Realty
        Designer: Ron Matteson

8946   Wallace Minner
        Designer: Ron Matteson

8947   Minner Inc.
        Designer: Ron Matteson

8948   Pro/Am Mini Sport Games
        Designer: Ron Matteson

8949   Blox
        Designer: Ron Matteson

8950   Earth Signs
        Designer: Ron Matteson

8951   P.D.O.P.S.
        Designer: Ron Matteson

8952   Employment Consultants
        Designer: Ron Matteson

8953   Grafiks Two
        Designer: Ron Matteson

8954   G.W. & Y. Advertising & p.r.
        Designer: Ron Matteson

8955   Hoag's Catering Service
        Designer: Lanny Sommese

8954

gibbons·wilson·young

ADVERTISING   PUBLIC RELATIONS INC.

8955

H·O·A·G'S
CATERING
SERVICE

8956

8957

8958

8959

8960

8961

8962

8963

8964

8965

8966

8956   Altoona Arts Festival
         Designer: Lanny Sommese

8957   Penn State University
         Designer: Lanny Sommese

8958   Women's Soccer League
         Designer: Lanny Sommese

8959   Sino-American Art Seminar
         Designer: Lanny Sommese

8960   Central Pennsylvania Festival
         of The Arts
         Designer: Lanny Sommese

8961   Central Pennsylvania Festival
         of The Arts
         Designer: Lanny Sommese

8962   Central Pennsylvania Festival
         of The Arts
         Designer: Lanny Sommese

8963   Central Pennsylvania Festival
         of The Arts
         Designer: Lanny Sommese

8964   Lemont Garage Secretarial Services
         (proposed)
         Designer: Lanny Sommese

8965   Lemont Garage Secretarial Services
         (proposed)
         Designer: Lanny Sommese

8966   Lemont Garage Secretarial Services
         Designer: Lanny Sommese

8967   Joseph Sommese Junk Dealer
         Designer: Lanny Sommese

8967

8968

8972

8969

8973

8970

8974

8971

8975

8976

8977

8978

8979

8968 Garry McShea Construction Co.
        Designer: Lanny Sommese

8969 Garry McShea Construction Co.
        (proposed)
        Designer: Lanny Sommese

8970 Garry McShea Construction Co.
        Designer: Larry Sommese

8971 The Press Box
        Designer: Lanny Sommese

8972 Ralph Licastro
        (Proposed)
        Designer: Lanny Sommese

8973 Ralph Licastro
        (proposed)
        Designer: Lanny Sommese

8974 Ralph Licastro
        (proposed)
        Designer: Lanny Sommese

8975 Joel Confer
        Designer: Lanny Sommese

8976 Joel Confer
        (proposed)
        Designer: Lanny Sommese

8977 International Assurance, Inc.
        Designer: Izhar Zik

8978 Storm Opinion Center
        Designer: Izhar Zik

8979 Technics in Design
        Designer: Izhar Zik

8980

8984

8981

8985

8982

8986

8983

8987

8988

8989

8990

8991

8980 The Graphics Gourmet
      Designer: Izhar Zik

8981 Atara Designs, Inc.
      Designer: Izhar Zik

8982 Insurance Institute For Research
      Designer: Izhar Zik

8983 In The Beginning
      Designer: Izhar Zik

8984 Quick Test, Inc.
      Designer: Izhar Zik

8985 Zik Jewelry
      Designer: Izhar Zik

8986 Northern Nuts & Bolts Co.
      Designer: Izhar Zik

8987 Dalia
      Designer: Izhar Zik

8988 Homsi, Inc.
      Designer: Izhar Zik

8989 Personal International Courier
          Service
      Designer: Izhar Zik

8990 ADM Industries, Inc.
      Designer: Izhar Zik

8991 Interstate Planning Association
      Designer: Izhar Zik

8992

8996

8993

LESNEY

ELECTRONICS

8997

8994

8998

8995

8999

9001

9002

9003

8992 Vision Network Affiliates, Inc.
Designer: Izhar Zik

8993 Lesney Electronics
Designer: Izhar Zik

8994 Vener Enterprises
Designer: Izhar Zik

8995 LSD Interior Decorators
Designer: Izhar Zik

8996 Visual Scene, Inc.
Designer: Izhar Zik

8997 Videoland
Designer: Izhar Zik

8998 The Lab
Designer: Luis Gonzalez
    Graphic Concepts

8999 Circle Seven Communications
Designer: Luis Gonzalez
    Graphic Concepts

9000 On-Line Property Managers
Designer: Luis Gonzalez
    Graphic Concepts

9001 Westgate Center
Designer: Luis Gonzalez
    Graphic Concepts

9002 Drillin' Rig
Designer: Luis Gonazlez
    Graphic Concepts

9003 Lamp-Lite Plus
Designer: Luis Gonzalez
    Graphic Concepts

9004

interior impressions

9008

COURTYARD

INTERIORS

9005

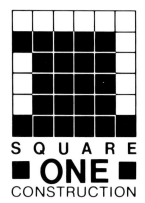

S Q U A R E
■ ONE ■
CONSTRUCTION

9009

COURTYARD

ANTIQUES

9006

CHAMBER
OF
COMMERCE
BRYAN / COLLEGE STATION, TX

9010

COURTYARD

GALLERY

9007

9011

COURTYARD

CLASSICS

T·H·E

DOCTOR'S OFFICE

9012

9013

9004   Interior Impressions
       Designer: Luis Gonzalez
         Graphic Concepts

9005   Square One Construction
       Designer: Luis Gonzalez
         Graphic Concepts

9006   Bryan-College Station Chamber
         of Commerce
       Designer: Ron Martin
         Graphic Concepts

9007   Texas Real Estate Research Center
       Designer: Ron Martin
         Graphic Concepts

9008   Courtyard Interiors
       Designer: Celia Jeter
         Graphic Concepts

9009   Courtyard Antiques
       Designer: Celia Jeter
         Graphic Concepts

9014

9010   Courtyard Gallery
       Designer: Celia Jeter
         Graphic Concepts

9011   Courtyard Classics
       Designer: Celia Jeter
         Graphic Concepts

9012   The Doctor's Office
       Designer: Celia Jeter
         Graphic Concepts

9013   Athletic Computer Programs
       Designer: Joni McGee
         Graphic Concepts

9015

9014   Down to Earth
       Designer: Joe Denton
         Graphic Concepts

9015   The Design Company
       Designer: Bob Zarwell

9016

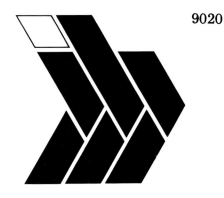

9020

9017

9021

9018

9022

9019

9023

9024

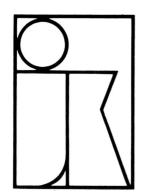

9025

9026

9027

9016   1976 Popai Exhibit
        Designer: Bob Zarwell

9017   Vulcan Industries Corporation
        Designer: Bob Zarwell

9018   Prestige Management Inc.
        Designer: Bob Zarwell

9019   Greater Milwaukee Open
        Designer: Bob Zarwell

9020   Institute of Health Management
        Designer: Bob Zarwell

9021   Funway Holidays
        Designer: Bob Zarwell

9022   Ridgeway Realty Inc.
        Designer: Bob Zarwell

9023   Midwest Business Brokers
        Designer: Bob Zarwell

9024   J-K Art Directions
        Designer: Bob Zarwell

9025   Americanway Carwash Systems Inc.
          (proposed)
        Designer: Bob Zarwell

9026   Line Tone Litho Inc.
        Designer: Bob Zarwell

9027   Kingshead Stylists
        Designer: Bob Zarwell

9028

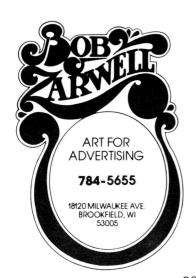

ART FOR
ADVERTISING

784-5655

18120 MILWAUKEE AVE.
BROOKFIELD, WI
53005

9031

9029

9032

9030

9033

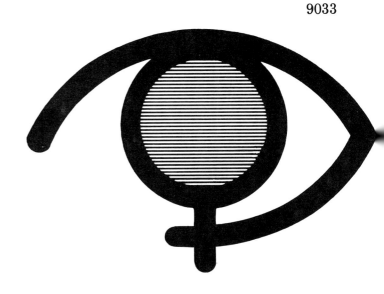

9034

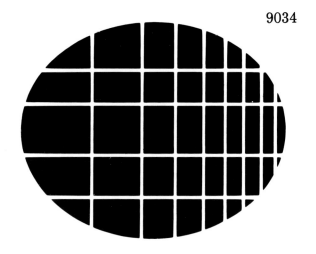

9028 Bob Zarwell
      Designer: Bob Zarwell

9029 Diversified Management Co.
      Designer: Cats' Pajamas

9030 Women's Independent Film Festival
      Designer: Cats' Pajamas

9031 Cats' Pajamas
      Designer: Cats' Pajamas

9032 Cooperating Fund Drive
      Designer: Cats' Pajamas

9033 Iris Video
      Designer: Cats' Pajamas

9034 EarthTech
      Designer: Valerie Kutchey

9035 TeleArts
      Designer: Valerie Kutchey

9036 The Westrend Group
        of the Trend Report
      Designer: P.J. Kelly

9035

9036

9037

9041

9038

9042

BLACK HAWK COUNTY ENERGY CONGRESS

9039

9043

9040

9044

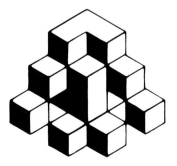

9045

9046

9047

9048

9037   Learning Trends
       Designer: P.J. Kelly

9038   Interserv Management Services
       Designer: P.J. Kelly

9039   Peoples Mutual Savings and Loan
       Designer: Robert Hellman
            Hellman Design Assoc.,Inc.

9040   Champion Advertising
       Designer: Tom Roper
            Hellman Design Assoc., Inc.

9041   Tom R Roper
       Designer:Tom Roper
            Hellman Design Assoc., Inc.

9042   Black Hawk County Energy Congress
       Designer: Tom Roper
            Hellman Design Assoc., Inc.

9043   Schoenfeld Clinical Laboratory
       Designer: Kim Behm
            Hellman Design Assoc., Inc.

9044   Reed and Association
       Designer: Kim Behm
            Hellman Design Assoc., Inc.

9045   Jan Jacobson Photography
       Designer: Kim Behm
            Hellman Design Assoc., Inc.

9046   Hellman Design Associates, Inc.
       Designer: Gary Gersema
            Hellman Design Assoc., Inc.

9047   Technical Assistance Program
       Designer: Gary Gersema
            Hellman Design Assoc., Inc.

9048   Thermal Corporation
       Designer: Gary Gersema
            Hellman Design Assoc., Inc.

9049

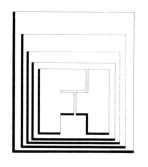

9053

9050

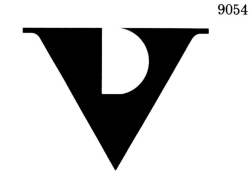

9054

9051

9055

9052

9056

9057

9058

9059

9060

9049 First Holding Corporation
      Designer: Gary Gersema
          Hellman Design Assoc., Inc.

9050 Perpetual Savings and Loan Assoc.
      Designer: Gary Gersema
          Hellman Design Assoc., Inc.

9051 Walker's Water
      Designer: Christopher C. Henneman

9052 Feminist Counselors
      Designer: Christopher C. Henneman

9053 Retail Advertising Seminar 1982
      Designer: Christopher C. Henneman

9054 Dominick Valenti
      Designer: Christopher C. Henneman

9055 Christopher C. Henneman
      Designer: Christopher C. Henneman

9056 Britton Racing Group
      Designer: 5 Penguins Design, Inc.

9057 Chuck Alton Productions
      Designer: 5 Penguins Design, Inc.

9058 Datatree
      Designer: 5 Pengrins Design, Inc.

9059 California Fine Arts Atelier
      Designer: 5 Penguins Design, Inc.

9060 Self Care Products, Inc.
      Designer: 5 Penguins Design, Inc.

9061

9062

9064

9063

9065

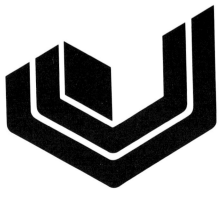

The Left Bank

9066

9067

9061 The Media Project
      Designer: 5 Penguins Design, Inc.

9062 Cambridge Graphics
      Designer: 5 Penguins Design, Inc.

9063 Stathem Smiles Cabinetmakers
      Designer: Mark Barensfeld

9064 WGUC
      Designer: Mark Barensfeld

9065 Cargoliner
      Designer: Mark Barensfeld

9066 The Left Bank Cafe Inc.
      Designer: D. Bruce Zahor
          & Joel Mitnick

9067 Aptick Printing Inc.
      Designer: D. Bruce Zahor
          & Joel Mitnick

9068 Hypnosis Training Institute
      Designer: D. Bruce Zahor

9069 The Art Director's Club of N.Y.
      Designer: D. Bruce Zahor

9068

9069

9070

9074

9071

9075

9072

9076

9073

9077

9078

9079

9080

9081

Learning Resource Center

9070   Bechet's Restaurant Inc.
       Designer: D. Bruce Zahor

9071   Pompizoo Restaurant
       Designer: D. Bruce Zahor

9072   Jaqueline Smith, Ph. D.
       Designer: D. Bruce Zahor

9073   New York City Housing
          Development Corp.
       Designer: D. Bruce Zahor

9074   Apple Bingo Supplies
       Designer: D. Bruce Zahor

9075   "Selling Artist Materials "
          A.J. Wildman & Son, Inc.
       Designer: D. Bruce Zahor

9076   Grand Central Racquetball Club Inc.
       Designer: D. Bruce Zahor

9077   Apro Systems Inc.
       Designer: D. Bruce Zahor

9078   New York City Dep. of Parks
          and Recreation
       Designer: D. Bruce Zahor

9079   Leif Hope's Laundry Restaurant Inc.
       Designer: D. Bruce Zahor

9080   Progressive Grocer Co.
       Designer: D. Bruce Zahor

9081   Learning Resource Center, American
          Express Co.
       Designer: D. Bruce Zahor

9082

9086

9083

9087

9084

9088

9085

9089

ASPEC

9090

9091

Qually & Company, Inc

9092

9082 International Womens's Writing
Guild
Designer: D. Bruce Zahor

9083 "A Choice in Therapy" Inc.
Designer: D. Bruce Zahor

9084 The Learning Store Ltd.
Designer: D. Bruce Zahor

9085 Tenth House Enterprises Inc.
Designer: D. Bruce Zahor

9086 Command Travel Inc.
Designer: D. Bruce Zahor

9087 The Design Group, Inc.
D. Bruce Zahor

9088 Gambetta's Pizza
Designer: Gambetta-Bollmer
Graphic Design

9089 ASPEC Product Dev. Corp.
Designer: Gambetta-Bollmer
Graphic Design

9090 Cornell Forge Company
Designer: Robert Qually

9091 Qually & Company, Inc.
Designer: Robert Qually

9092 New Archery Products
Designer: Conrad Fialkowski

9093 Daily Planet
Designer: Conrad Fialdowski

9093

9094

9097

9095

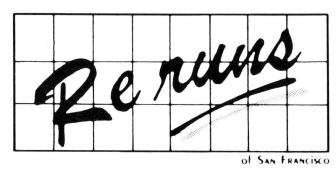

of San Francisco

9096

KINROW
ESTATES

9099

9100

9101

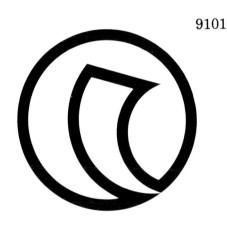

9094   Olsen's Day Care Center
        Designer: David Bullock

9095   Twin Jesters Restaurant
        Designer: David Bullock

9096   Kinrow Estates
        Designer: David Bullock

9097   R. Seth Vorisek
        Designer: R. Seth Vorisek

9098   ReRuns of San Francisco
        Designer: R. Seth Vorisek

9099   ReRuns of San Francisco
        Designer: R. Seth Vorisek

9100   Peter Dechar
        Designer: Tree Trapanese

9101   Chinese Christian Herald Crusades
        Designer: Andy Lun

9102   Union Process, Inc.
        Designer: P.R. Assoc., Inc.

9102

Union process

9103

9107

CASHCO

9108

COMPUTER SHOWCASE

9104

ADA

9105

Olympia Centre

9109

WESTSIDE
COMMERCIAL BROKERAGE COMPANY

9110

KELLER

9106

DYNAQUEST

9111

9112

9113

9103 Metropolitan Hand Center
      Designer: Mary Beth Bostrum Cybul
         Hill and Knowlton, Inc.

9104 ADA
      Designer: Mary Beth Bostrum Cybul
         Hill and Knowlton, Inc.

9105 Olympia & York
      Designer: Mark Tendam
         Hill and Knowlton, Inc.

9106 Dynaquest
      Designer: Greg Scott
         Hill and Knowlton, Inc.

9107 Cashco
      Designer: Greg Scott
         Hill and Knowlton, Inc.

9108 Computer Showcase
      Designer: Phyllis Persechini
         Persechini & Moss

9109 Westside Commercial Brokerage Co.
      Designer: Phyllis Persechini
         Persechini & Moss

9110 Keller Construction Company
      Designer: Phyllis Persechini
         Persechini & Moss

9111 Young Musicians Foundation
      Designer: Shannon Heiman
         Persechini & Moss

9112 Westside Towers
      Designer: Shannon Heiman
         Persechini & Moss

9113 Yarbrough and Company
      Designer: Shannon Heiman
         Persechini & Moss

9114

9115

9116

9117

9114   Hotel Air Sands
       Designer: Shannon Heiman
         Persechini & Moss

9115   The Lone Ranger
       Designer: Shannon Heiman
         Persechini & Moss

9116   Giarnella Design
       Designer: Giarnella Design

9117   Graphic Dimensions
       Designer: Giarnella Design

9118   Graphic Dimensions
       Designer: Giarnella Design

9118

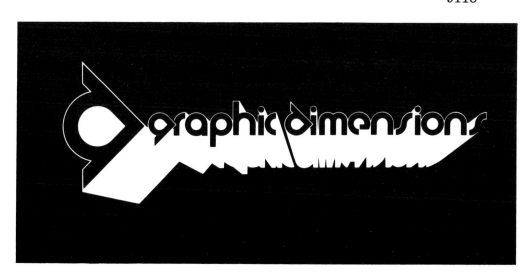

9119

9123

Tyrol & Mikan

9120

9124

9121

9125

HYPNOSIS PLUS

9122

COMBUSTION TECHNOLOGΔES

9126

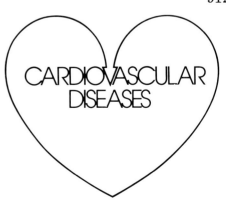

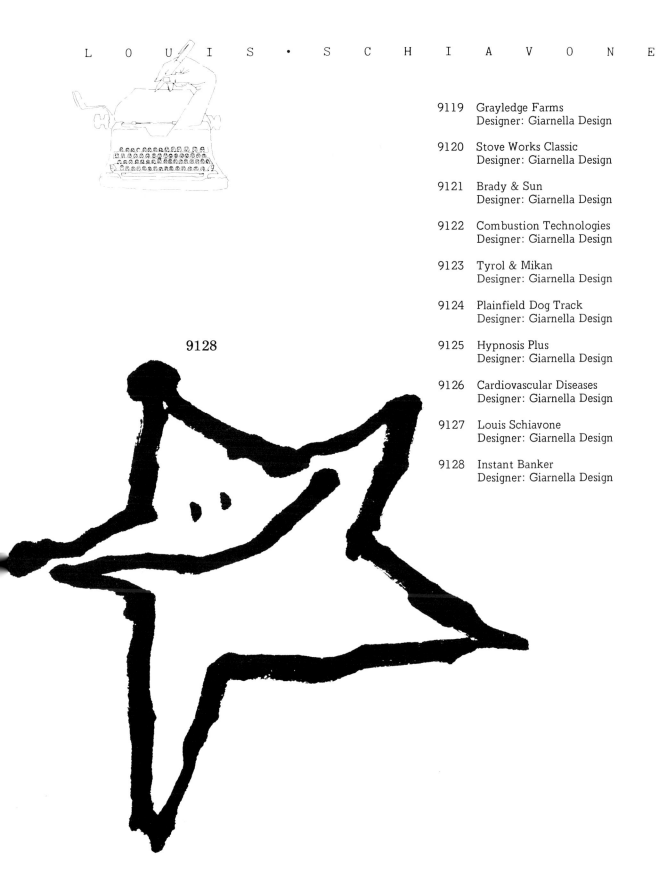

9128

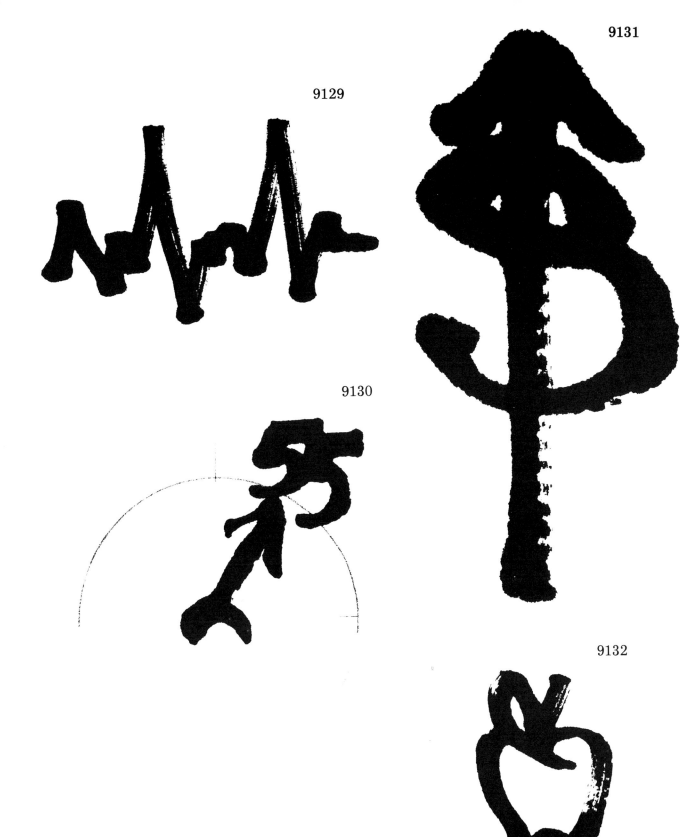

9129

9131

9130

9132

Advanced Group Life  Health Insurance

9134

9135

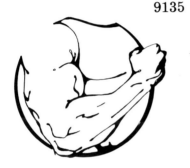

9136

9137

9129   Aetna Life and Casualty Co.
       Designer: Giarnella Design

9130   Aetna Life and Casualty Co.
       Designer: Giarnella Design

9131   Aetna Life and Casualty Co.
       Designer: Giarnella Design

9132   Aetna Life and Casualty Co.
       Designer: Giarnella Design

9133   Aetna Life and Casualty Co.
       Designer: Giarnella Design

9134   Aetna Life and Casualty Co.
       Designer: Giarnella Design

9135   Aetna Life and Casualty Co.
       Designer: Giarnella Design

9136   Aetna Life and Casualty Co.
       Designer: Giarnella Design

9137   Aetna Life and Casualty Co.
       Designer: Giarnella Casualty Co.

9138

9142

9139

9143

9140

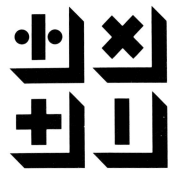

9144

Hettig
& Company

9141

9145

9146

The Ashford Group, Inc.

9147

9148

9138 H.A. Stroh Assoc., Inc.
Designer: Stephen Longo & Assoc.

9139 Nabisco
Designer: Stephen Longo & Assoc.

9140 Fersko, Wasilewski and Company
Designer: Stephen Longo & Assoc.

9141 Stephen Longo
Designer: Stephen Longo & Assoc.

9142 Nabisco
Designer: Stephen Longo & Assoc.

9143 Gulf Houston Properties, Inc.
Designer: Rosalie Ramsden

9144 Hettig & Co.
Designer: Rosalie Ramsden

9145 YWCA of Houston
Designer: Rosalie Ramsden

9146 The Ashford Group
Designer: Rosalie Ramsden

9147 Professional Women in Agriculture
Designer: Rosalie Ramsden

9148 The Museum of Printing History
Designer: Rosalie Ramsden

9149 Astron Energy Corporation
Designer: Scott Engen

9149

9150

9154

9151

9155

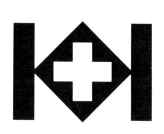

9152

9156

9153

9157

9158

SPORTSAM

9159

9160

9161

9150 Investigations, Ltd.
Designer: Scott Engen

9151 Gamesman
Designer: Scott Engen

9152 Childrens Dance Workshop
Designer: Scott Engen

9153 Parking Services
Designer: Scott Engen

9154 Printmakers
Designer: Scott Engen

9155 Pens V
Designer: Scott Engen

9156 K+K Medical Supply
Designer: Scott Engen

9157 Associated Students of the
University of Utah
Designer: Scott Engen

9158 Sports Am
Designer: Scott Engen

9159 Rowmark Ski Academy
Designer: Scott Engen

9160 Solitude Ski Team
Designer: Scott Engen

9161 Scott Engen, Ski Coach
Designer: Scott Engen

9162

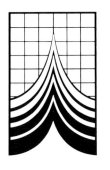

9166

9163

9167

9164

9168

9165

9169

9170

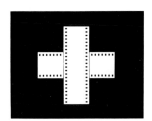

9171

9172

9173

9162 Lone Peak Food and Beverage Inc.
      Designer: Scott Engen

9163 Marcus Grant Advertising
      Designer: Scott Engen

9164 Vine Lore
      Designer: Scott Engen

9165 Creative Communications Consulting
          Company
      Designer: Scott Engen

9166 Graphic Concepts, Inc.
      Designer: Scott Engen

9167 Lancaster Limited
      Designer: Scott Engen

9168 Guadalupe Center of Salt Lake City
      Designer: Scott Engen

9169 Diamond Tree Branch
      Designer: Scott Engen

9170 Swiss Film Festival
      Designer: Scott Engen

9171 Quadrant
      Designer: Scott Engen

9172 International Applied Sciences Inc.
      Designer: Benjamin R. Larrabee

9173 Damon Corporation
      Designer: Benjamin R. Larrabee

9174

American
Made

9178

9175

ARNOLD PECK REALTY

9179

9176

AVIATION
TRAINING SERVICES

9180

9177

PPE
ASSOCIATES, INC.

9181

9182

9174 Jerry Sharan Graphics
       Designer: Susanne Bordeau
         Jerry Sharan Graphics

9175 Arnold Peck Realty
       Designer: Susanne Bordeau
         Jerry Sharan Graphics

9176 Aviation Training Services
       Designer: Susanne Bordeau
         Jerry Sharan Graphics

9177 Pilot Proficiency Examiners
       Association, Inc.
       Designer: Jerry Sharan
         Sharan Graphics

9178 Mid-American Dance Company
       Designer: Dennis Ichiyama

9179 University Design Organization
       (proposal)
       Designer: Dennis Ichiyama

9180 The Monet Trio
       Designer: Dennis Ichiyama

9181 Weidlinger Associates
       Designer: George Tscherny

9182 Montgomery Communications, Inc.
       Designer: George Tscherny

9183 The Light Opera of Manhattan
       Designer: George Tscherny

9184 Ernst & Whinney
       Designer: George Tscherny

9183

9184

9185

9188

9186

9189

Greystone

9187

9190

9191

9192

9193

9185 Bender Management Consultants Inc.
      Designer: George Tscherny

9186 Fidelity Group of Funds
      Designer: George Tscherny

9187 Roto-Rooter
      Designer: George Tscherny

9188 SEi Trust Funds
      Designer: George Tscherny

9189 Greystone
      Designer: Jean-Claude Muller
          John Follis & Assoc.

9190 Dharmala
      Designer: Jean-Claude Muller
          John Follis & Assoc.

9191 Gajah Mada Plaza
      Designer: Joe Stoddard
          John Follis & Assoc.

9192 Converse Davis Dixon
      Designer: Joe Stoddard
          John Follis & Assoc.

9193 Panda Inn
      Designer: Connie Beck

9194

Springfield MUTUAL Inc.

9198

The St Nicholas

9195

 **RALPH HAHN AND ASSOCIATES**
CONSULTING AND DESIGN ENGINEERS INC.

9199

ANDREWS ENVIRONMENTAL
ENGINEERING INC.

9196

**Illinois
Department of
Revenue**

9200

 **the
Graduat
School**
of
Hair
Design

9197

Illinois
State Board of
Education

920

KokeMil

9202

Citizens Savings and Loan Association

9203

9194 Springfield Mutual Realtors
Designer: Com Unigraph Inc.

9195 Ralph Hahn and Associates
Designer: Con Unigraph Inc.

9196 Illinois Department of Revenue
Designer: Com Unigraph Inc.

9197 Illinois State Board of Education
Designer: Com Unigraph Inc.

9198 St. Nicholas Apartments
Designer: Com Unigraph Inc.

9199 Andrews Environmental
Engineering Inc.
Designer: Com Unigraph Inc.

9200 The Graduate School of Hair Design
Designer: Com Unigraph Inc.

9201 Kokemill Development
Designer: Com Unigraph Inc.

9202 Citizens Savings and Loan Assoc.
Designer: Com Unigraph Inc.

9203 Springfield Central Area
Development Association
Designer: Com Unigraph Inc.

9204 BiPetro
Designer: Com Unigraph Inc.

9205 Lithocrest Printing
Designer: Com Unigraph Inc.

9204

9205

 LITHOCREST

9206

 **CONVOCOM**

9207

M.G.Nelson
Builder / Developer / Realtor

9208

St. Mary's Hospital

9209

 **Firstbank of Illinois Co.**

9210

Dixon
Bretscher
Noonan, Inc.

9211

9206 Convocom Telecommunications
      Designer: Com Unigraph Inc.

9207 M.G. Nelson
      Designer: Com Unigraph Inc.

9208 St. Mary's Hospital
      Designer: Com Unigraph Inc.

9209 Firstbank of Illinois Co.
      Designer: Com Unigraph Inc.

9210 Dixon Bretscher Noonan, Inc.
      Designer: Com Unigraph Inc.

9211 Lincolnfest
      Designer: Com Unigraph Inc.

9212 St. Joseph's Hospital
      Designer: Com Unigraph Inc.

9212

St Joseph's Hospital

9213

9217

DOCTOR'S HOUSE CALL
— for pets —

9214

9218

PENGUIN · PRODUCTIONS

9215

9219

9216

9220

The Ultimate Street Skate

9221

9222

9223

9224

murphy·roth

9225

SKIResearch

9229

WRRalls

COMPANY

9226

Verne Pershing

FILM PRODUCTIONS

9230

SKI REFLECTIONS

9227

Mother's BAR & GRILLE

9231

Tim Baker

CONTRACTORS · DEVELOPERS

9228

Tennis Agents
International

9232

Graphics Unlimited
LITHOGRAPHY

9233

9234

9235

9236

9240

YOUTH THEATRE GUILD

9237

9241

ALBERT MARDIKIAN
ENGINEERING

9238

RADIANCE

9242

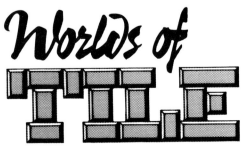

9239

9243

EXECUTIVE COACHCRAFT

9245

9246

CANTERBURY INN

9247

9236	Solargas	Designer: Michael Faye
9237	Chef's Pollo	Designer: Michael Faye
9238	Cosmetic Development Systems	Designer: Michael Faye
9239	Karlyn International	Designer: Michael Faye
9240	Youth Theatre Guild	Designer: Michael Faye
9241	Albert Mardikian Engineering	Designer: Michael Faye
9242	Linda Staehr	Designer: Michael Faye
9243	Worlds of Tile	Designer: Michael Faye
9244	Executive Coachcraft, Inc.	Designer: Michael Faye
9245	Sierra Spas	Designer: Michael Faye
9246	Canterbury Inn	Designer: Michael Faye
9247	The Glass Eye, Inc.	Designer: Michael Faye

9248

MUSIC & MEMORIES

9252

9249

california HI-LITES

9253

Coburn Consultants Inc

9254

9250

CALIFORNIA MINT

A Limited Edition Investment Company

9251

GEROLD & MILLS

REAL · ESTATE

925

THE PORTHOLE

9256

Manhattan Beach Education Foundation

9257

9258

9259

9260

9264

9261

9265

TECHNOLOGY
SYSTEMS
ORGANIZATION
INC.

9262

9266

9263

9267

9268

9269

9270

9260   Silver Shear Hair Design
       Designer: Michael Faye

9261   Computers, Et Cetera
       Designer: Michael Faye

9262   Republic Distributors, Inc.
       Designer: Machael Faye

9263   Hope Chapel
       Designer: Michael Faye

9264   Quoin Development Corp.
       Designer: Michael Faye

9265   Technology Systems
          Organization, Inc.
       Designer: Michael Faye

9266   Hook City Records
       Designer: Michael Faye

9267   Marquee Productions
       Designer: Michael Faye

9268   Anny's Hair Salon
       Designer: Michael Faye

9269   Palos Verdes Flooring Center
       Designer: Michael Faye

9270   Ascot Grand Prix
       Designer: Michael Faye

9271

Micro Linear

9275

9272

9276

AURICLE

9273

Fresh Western

MARKETING INC.

9277

Westminster Software

9274

M/\/\B

9278

GENESIS GROUP

9279

9280

COLUMBIA DIVERSIFIED ENERGIES, inc.

9281

9282

Professional Athletes Career Enterprises, Inc.

9271 Micro Linear
      Designer: Patty Richmond Design

9272 B & B Photography
      Designer: Patty Richmond Design

9273 Fresh Western, Inc.
      Designer: Patty Richmond Design

9274 McMillan, Moore, & Bucannan
          Real Estate
          (proposal)
      Designer: Patty Richmond Design

9275 Bruce Church, Inc.
      Designer: Patty Richmond Design

9276 Auricle
      Designer: Patty Richmond Design

9277 Westminster Software
      Designer: Patty Richmond Design

9278 Genesis Group
      Designer: Patty Richmond Design

9279 Adventist Health System
      Designer: Curt Hamilton
          Robert Brandt Advertising, Inc.

9280 Columbia Diversified Energies, Inc.
      Designer: Curt Hamilton
          Robert Brandt Advertising, Inc.

9281 Lakeside Steel Corporation
      Designer: Curt Hamilton
          Robert Brandt Advertising, Inc.

9282 Professional Athletes Career
          Enterprises, Inc.
      Designer: Curt Hamilton
          Robert Brandt Advertising, Inc.

9283

Hyde Park
Community Hospital

9284

THOREK
Hospital and
Medical Center

9285

9286

9287

9288

9289

9290

9291

9292

9283   Hyde Park Community Hospital
       Designer: Waldo Pacheco
          Robert Brandt Advertising. Inc.

9284   Thorek Hospital and Medical Center
       Designer: Waldo Pacheco
          Robert Brandt Advertising, Inc.

9285   Glendale Heights Community
          Hospital
       Designer: Waldo Pacheco
          Robert Brandt Advertising, Inc.

9286   Garvey Marketing Group
       Designer: Waldo Pacheco
          Robert Brandt Advertising, Inc.

9287   Good Deal & Co.
       Designer: Waldo Pacheco
          Robert Brandt Advertising, Inc.

9288   The Wood Specialists
       Designer: Waldo Pacheco
          Robert Brandt Advertising, Inc.

9289   New Day Centers
       Designer: Cynthia Radke
          Robert Brandt Advertising, Inc.

9290   The Pointe
       Designer: Ron Spielman
          Robert Brandt Advertising, Inc.

9291   John H. Harland Co.
       Designer: John H. Harland Co.

9292   Harland Planning Meeting
       Designer: John H. Harland Co.

9293   Skyview Graphics, Inc.
       Designer: Constance Kovar Graphic
          Design, Inc.

9293

9294

9295

Baker's Dozen

9297

warm, shaped cookies

9296

9298

Circular Screen

BROADCASTERS MEDIA SERVICES, INC.

9299

9300

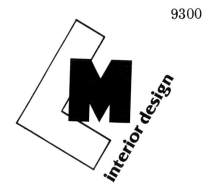

9301

9294   David Parker
       Designer: David Alexander Parker

9295   Baker's Dozen
       Designer: John K. Landis Graphic
          Design

9296   Circular Screen
       Designer: John K. Landis Graphic
          Design

9297   Sue Lindsey
       Designer: leAd Advertising & Design

9298   Potomac Inc.
       Designer: leAd Advertising & Design

9299   DRP Litho
       Designer: leAd Advertising & Design

9300   McArthur, Thomas
       Designer: leAd Advertising & Design

9301   Dave Rosencrans
       Designer: Mark Setteducatl Design

9302   John Battenberg
       Designer: Linda Fillhardt

9302

BATTENBERG

9303

DD ASSOCIATES INC

9307

INA CORPORATION

9304

birth

THE BIRTH
AND
FAMILY CENTER

9308

GANNETT

9305

Air National

9306

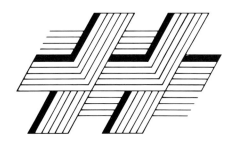

9309

DANNON®

CREAM OF WHEAT

9311

CHICOPEE

9303 DD Associates
Designer: Linda Fillhardt

9204 The Birth & Family Center
Designer: Linda Fillhardt

9305 Air National
Designer: Linda Fillhardt

9306 Holmes & Company
Designer: Linda Fillhardt

9307 INA Corporation
Designer: Yasumura/CYB

9308 Gannett
Designer: Yasumura/CYB

9309 Dannon
Designer: Yasumura/CYB

9310 Cream of Wheat
Designer: Yasumura/ CYB

9311 Chicopee
Designer: Yasumura/CYB

9312 USA Today
Designer: Yasumura/CYB

9312

USA TODAY

9313

WESTON

9314

9317

9315

9318

9316

9319

9320

9321

9322

9323

9313 Weston Instruments
      Designer: Yasumura/CYB

9314 Uniting Community Church
      Designer: Maria Mazzara

9315 Design Group M
      Designer: Maria Mazzara

9316 Electron Optics
      Designer: Maria Mazzara

9317 City of South St. Paul
      Designer: Maria Mazzara

9318 JoAnn Nicholson & Judy Lewis
      Designer: Maria Mazzara

9319 Maria Mazzara
      Designer: Maria Mazzara

9320 Central Security Insurance
      Designer: Maria Mazzara

9321 Mark Kawell
      Designer: Maria Mazzara

9322 Minnesota Pollution Control Agency
      Designer: Maria Mazzara

9323 Winston Press
      Designer: Maria Mazzara

9324

9328

9325

9329

9326

9330

9327

9331

9332

9333

9334

9335

9324 Studio Graphics
      Designer: Maria Mazzara

9325 Buck Hill Ski Racing Club
      Designer: Maria Mazzara

9326 Buck Hill Ski Racing Club
      Designer: Maria Mazzara

9327 Professional Development Programs
      Designer: Maria Mazzara

9328 Buckley's Ski Emporium
      Designer: Maria Mazzara

9329 Southwest Minnesota State College
      Designer: Maria Mazzara

9330 Persimmon Productions
      Designer: Maria Mazzara

9331 Design East
      Designer: Maria Mazzara

9332 Lindwood Forest Townhouses
      Designer: Maria Mazzara

9333 des Tasses Mug Shop
      Designer: Maria Mazzara

9334 Sandpebbles Gift Store
      Designer: Maria Mazzara

9335 American Israel Cultural Foundation
      Designer: Nanette Hucknall

9336

9337

9339

EUROCOM

9338

9340

ucc

NESS TORY TRAVEL CLUB 9341

9342

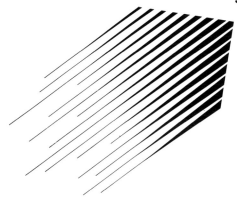

9343

9336   Women's Networking Committee
        UJA-Federation Campaign
        Designer: Nanette Hucknall

9337   The Jewish Theological Seminary
        of America
        Designer: Nanette Hucknall

9338   Jewish Reconstructionist Foundation
        Designer: Nanette Hucknall

9339   Eurocom
        Designer: Marvin Trull

9340   Veshima Coffee Co. Ltd.
        Designer: Jitsuo Hoashi

9341   Ness Tory Travel Club
        Designer: George McGinnis/
        David Parker

9342   Image Network
        Designer: George McGinnis/
        Susan Borgen

9343   Best Boy Feature Film
        Designer: George McGinnis/
        Lisa LLoyd

9344   WGN
        Designer: John Rea/
        George McGinnis

9344

9345

9349

9346

9350

9347

9351

9348

9352

9353

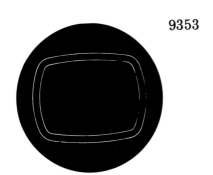

9354

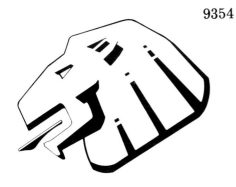

9355

Middle East Television

9356

9345 WGN
Designer: John Rea/
George McGinnis

9346 WGN
Designer: John Rea/
George McGinnis

9347 WPIX New York
Designer: John Rea/
George McGinnis

9348 Showtime Entertainment
Designer: John Rea/
George McGinnis

9349 Channel 25 Boston
Designer: John Rea/
George McGinnis

9350 Channel 25 Boston
Designer: John Rea/
George McGinnis

9351 Paramount Pictures
Designer: John Rea/
George McGinnis

9352 Showtime Entertainment
Designer: George McGinnis

9353 Showtime Entertainment
Designer: George McGinnis

9354 T.V. Radio Caracas
Designer: George McGinnis

9355 Christian Broadcasting Television
Designer: George McGinnis

9356 Institute of French Petroleum
Designer: George McGinnis

9357

9361

9358

9362

9359

9363

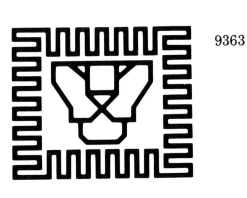

9360

9364

9365

LesHalles
NEW YORK

9366

9367

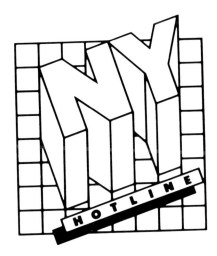

9357	Corinthian Broadcasting Corporation Designer: George McGinnis
9358	Corinthian Broadcasting Corporation Designer: George McGinnis
9359	Corinthian Broadcasting Corporation Designer: George McGinnis
9360	Corinthian Broadcasting Corporation Designer: George McGinnis
9361	Japan Chemical Shoes Industry Association Inc. Designer: Jitsuo Hoashi
9362	The Seiyu Stores Co. Limited Designer: Jitsuo Hoashi
9363	Club "E" Nightclub Designer: Jitsuo Hoashi
9364	Grouse Run, Inc. Designer: Jitsuo Hoashi
9365	Les Halles Designer: Jitsuo Hoashi
9366	Reduta Deux Theatrical Co. Designer: Jitsuo Hoashi
9367	Fashion Store "Zero One" Designer: Jitsuo Hoashi
9368	Art Directors Club Designer: Jitsuo Hoashi

9368

9369

9373

9370

9374

9371

9375

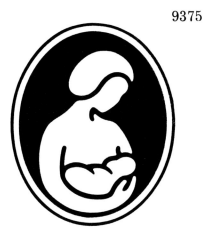

9372

9376

9377

9378

9379

9380

9369   Christian Broadcasting Network
        Designer: Jitsuo Hoashi

9370   Veshima Coffee Co.
        Designer: Jitsuo Hoashi

9371   Morozoff Limited
        Designer: Jitsuo Hoashi

9372   Sutton Creek Partnership
        Designer: Wayne Kosterman
            Assoc., Inc.

9373   Saint Joseph Hospital
        Designer: Wayne Kosterman
            Assoc., Inc.

9374   Premier Banks, Inc.
        Designer: Wayne Kosterman
            Assoc., Inc.

9375   La Leche League International
        Designer: Wayne Kosterman
            Assoc., Inc.

9376   Minor Emergency Centers, Inc.
        Designer: Wayne Kosterman
            Assoc., Inc.

9377   Americor Enterprises, Inc.
        Designer: Wayne Kosterman
            Assoc., Inc.

9378   School District 54
        Designer: Wayne Kosterman
            Assoc., Inc.

9379   Bolingbrook Medical Center
        Designer: Wayne Kosterman
            Assoc., Inc.

9380   Village of Roselle
        Designer:Wayne Kosterman
            Assoc., Inc.

9381

9382

9383

QUIKFENCE

9384

LELAND MUSIC

9385

9386

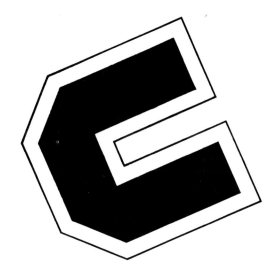

9381   Alpha Graphix
      Designer: The Weller Institute

9382   Quickfence
      Designer: The Weller Institute

9383   Studio International
      Designer: The Weller Institute

9384   Leland Music
      Designer: The Weller Institute

9385   Dentsu, Inc.
      Designer: H.L. Chu & Co. Ltd.

9386   The Cooper Union
      Designer: H.L. Chu & Co. Ltd.

9387   Heather Evans Incorporated
      Designer: H.L. Chu & Co. Ltd.

9387

9388

9390

9389

9391

9392

SUN TOURS INC

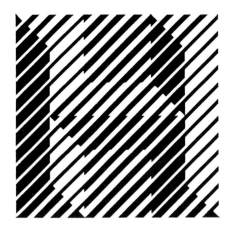

9393

9394

9395

9388 Winsor Dental Studio
      Designer: H.L. Chu & Co. Ltd.

9389 New York University Medical Center
          Blood Program
      Designer: H.L.Chu & Co. Ltd.

9390 Pellegrini & Kaestle, Inc.
      Designer: H.L. Chu & Co. Ltd.

9391 Press Brenner Communications, Inc.
      Designer: H.L. Chu & Co.
      Designer: H.L. Chu & Co. Ltd.

9392 Sun Tours Inc.
      Designer: H.L.Chu & Co. Ltd.

9393 A.L. Havens Securities, Inc.
      Designer: H.L. Chu & Co. Ltd

9394 Polk's Hobbies
      Designer: H.L. Chu & Co. Ltd.

9395 Hoi Ling Chu
      Designer: H.L. Chu & Co. Ltd.

9396

9401

9397

9402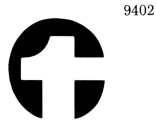

9398

9403

9399

9404

9405

9400

9406

9407

9408

9409

9396   Equestrian Centers of America, Inc.
Designer: Rose Farber

9397   Elaine Goldy Properties
Designer: Rose Farber

9398   San Fernando Community
Designer: Rose Farber

9399   BBC International
Designer: Rose Farber

9400   Western Technologies, Inc.
Designer: Rose Farber

9401   Aspen Hill
Designer: Rose Farber

9402   First Capital Partners, Inc.
Designer: Rose Farber

9403   Brentwood Energy
Designer: Rose Farber

9404   The Crystal Fountain Restaurant
Designer: Rose Farber

9405   Century General Corporation
Designer: Rose Farber

9406   Camseal Inc.
Designer: Rose Farber

9407   Sunset Summit Condominiums
Designer: Rose Farber

9408   American Capital Investors, Inc.
Designer: Rose Farber

9409   Corsair Asset Management, Inc.
Designer: Rose Farber

9410

9413

9411

9414

9412

SKY
TIGER

9415

9416

9417

9410   Balloons Instead
        Designer: Eugene Cheltenham

9411   California Mart
        Designer: Eugene Cheltenham

9412   Spectra Star Kites
        Designer: Eugene Cheltenham

9413   Sun King
        Designer: Eugene Cheltenham

9414   Right Side of the Brain/Seminar
        Designer: Eugene Cheltenham

9415   Skatey's
        Designer: Eugene Cheltenham

9416   California Mart
        Designer: Eugene Cheltenham

9417   Literary Women
        Designer: Eugene Cheltenham

9418   Jack Loeb Printing Production
        Designer: Eugene Cheltenham

9419   Kendra Kollectables
        Designer: Eugene Cheltenham

9418

9419

9420

© 1980 L.A. Olympic Committee   TM

9421

9422

9420 Games of the XXIII Olympiad
      Los Angeles 1984
      Designer: Robert Miles Runyan
      & Associates

9421 Southern California Savings
      Designer: Robert Miles Runyan
      & Associates

9422 SARSA
      Designer: Robert Miles Runyan
      & Associates

9423 Obunsha Publishing Co., Ltd.
      Designer: Robert Miles Runyan
      & Associates

9423

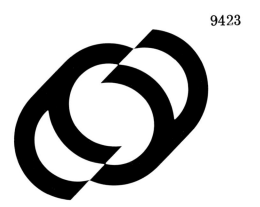

9424

9427

9425

9428

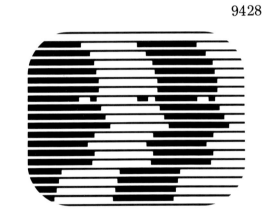

9426

9429

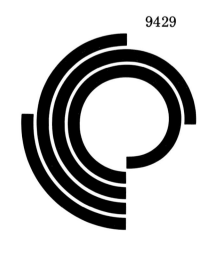

9430

9431

9432

9424 Unibanco, S.A.
Designer: Robert Miles Runyan
& Associates

9425 Los Coyotes Country Club
Designer: Robert Miles Runyan
& Associates

9426 Los Coyotes Country Club
Designer: Robert Miles Runyan
& Associates

9427 Vuarnet France
Designer: Robert Miles Runyan
& Associates

9428 Visual Marketing Associates
Designer: Robert Miles Runyan
& Associates

9429 Pharmavite
Designer: Robert Miles Runyan
& Associates

9430 Jerry Pavey Design
Designer: Jerry Pavey Design

9431 Nancy Barchas
Designer: Jerry Pavey Design

9432 Federal Farm Credit Board
Designer: Jerry Pavey Design

9433

COMMUNICATORS ORIENTATION
WASHINGTON, DC

9437

9434

The 25th
Anniversary
Federal Farm
Credit Board

9438

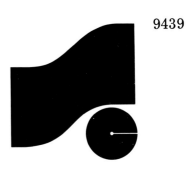

Tia Queta

9435

9439

9436

Quarterly
The Fiscal Agency Of The Farm
Credit Banks
Review

9440

TEAMWORK: NOW, TOMORROW

9241

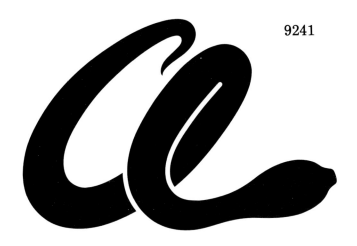

9442

9443

9433   Farm Credit Administration
       Designer: Jerry Pavey Design

9434   Federal Farm Credit Board
       Designer: Jerry Pavey Design

9435   Farm Credit Administration
       Designer: Jerry Pavey Design

9436   The Fiscal Agency for the
          Farm Credit Board
       Designer: Jerry Pavey Design

9437   Federal Farm Credit Board
       Designer: Jerry Pavey Design

9438   Tia Queta Mexican Restaurant
       Designer: Jerry Pavey Design

9439   Svec/ Conway Printers
       Designer: Jerry Pavey Design

9440   The American Institute
          of Cooperation
       Designer: Jerry Pavey Design

9441   Arntz Cobra
       Designer: Marty Neumeier

9442   Summit University
       Designer: Marty Neumeier

9443   Avant Cards
       Designer: Marty Neumeier

9444

9447

9445

9448

9446

PAPERBOOKS

9449

9450

9451

9444 Educational Video
Designer: Marty Neumeier

9445 Chroma Litho
Designer: Marty Neumeier

9446 Paperbooks, Inc.
Designer: Marty Neumeier
& Kathleen Trainor Joynes

9447 Kings West
Designer: Marty Neumier
& Byron Glaser

9448 Western Medical
Designer: Marty Neumeier

9449 Creative Education
Designer: Marty Neumeier

9450 U.S. Invest
Designer: Marty Neumeier
& Sandra Higashi

9451 Edward deBono School of Thinking
Designer: Marty Neumeier

9452 Eatz Restaurants
Designer: Marty Neumeier

9452

9453

9457

9454

9458

9455

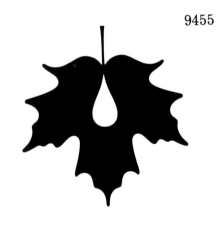

9459

9456

9460

9461

9462

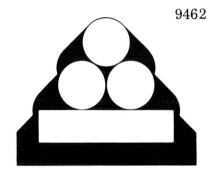

9463

9464

9453   Casper Events Center
        Designer: Communication Arts Inc.

9454   Medical Management Group
        Designer: Communication Arts Inc.

9455   Babiyar Park
        Designer: Communication Arts Inc.

9456   Monitor Maintenance
        Designer: Communication Arts Inc.

9457   Champion Cable Chain
        Designer: Communication Arts Inc.

9458   Potato Patch Club
        Designer: Communication Arts Inc.

9459   Medical Couriers
        Designer: Communication Arts Inc.

9460   Healthworks
        Designer: Communication Arts Inc.

9461   My Friends
        Designer: Communication Arts Inc.

9462   Hiroshi Kira
        Designer: Communication Arts Inc.

9463   Southwest
        Designer: Communication Arts Inc.

9464   Colorado Federal
        Designer: Communication Arts Inc.

Index of Marks

Designers

5 Penguins, Design; 269 W. Alameda Ave., Burbank, CA 91052

Adam, Filippo & Moran Inc.; Design Consultants, 1206 Fifth Ave., Pittsburgh, PA 15219

Adams, James M.; Adams Graphic Design Group, 106 S. McKinney, Richardson, TX 75081

Advance Design Center; 4020 Oak Lawn Ave., Dallas, TX 75219

Bass, Melanie; 1358 N. Cliff Valley Way N.E., Apt. D-5, Atlanta, GA 30319

Beer, Henry; Communication Arts Incorporated, 1112 Pearl St., Boulder, CO 80302

Biles, William L.; Biles Design, 2990 Richmond, Suite 105, Houston, TX 77098

Brumfield, Debbie; D. Brumfield Design, 1314 W. Main St., Nacogdoches, TX 75961

Bullock, David & Nora; Graphic Design/ Illustration, 617 Luella Dr., Kutztown, PA 19530

Cats' Pajamas; 344 Ramsey, Saint Paul, MN 55102

Cheltenham, Eugene; 2224 Silver Ridge Ave., No. 4, Los Angeles, CA 90039

Chu, H.L., & Company Ltd; 39 W. 29 St., New York, NY 10001

Cohen, Emil M.; 2607 Kenilworth Ave., Wilmette, IL 60091

ComUnigraph Incorporated; 530 S. Grand West, Springfield, IL 62704

Connelly, Don; Don Donnelly & Associates, PO Box 536, 31 Avondale Plaza, Avondale Estates, GA 30002

Constance Kovar Graphic Design, Inc.; The General Design Store, 300 Woodbury Rd., Woodbury, NY 11797

Dellinger, Harvey; 39 McDaniel Ct., Greenville, SC 29605

Design Company, The; 12201 W. Burleigh, Milwaukee, WI 53222

Designed to Print, Inc,; 270 W. 73 St., New York, NY 10023

Dixon & Parcels Associates Inc.; 521 Fifth Ave., New York, NY 10017

Doremus & Company; Advertising/Public Relations, 850 N. Church St., Rockford, IL 61103

Engen, Scott; 9058 Greenhills Dr., Sandy, UT 84092

Engle, Ray, & Associates; 626 S. Kenmore, Los Angeles, CA 90005

English Finish Advertising Company Limited, The; 427 Woodlawn Ave., Cambridge, OH 43725

Farber; 385 S. End Ave., New York, NY 10280

Faye, Michael, Associates; 500 S. Sepulveda, Suite 304, Manhattan Beach, CA 90266

Ferraro, Armando S.; 3101-D Colonial Way, Atlanta, GA 30341

Fialkowski, Conrad; Suite 3260, 401 N. Michigan, Chicago, IL 60611

Fillhardt, Linda; Graphic Design, 236 N. Santa Cruz Ave., Suite 225A, Los Gatos, CA 95030

Follis Design; 2124 Venice Blvd., Los Angeles, CA 90006-5299

Forbes, F. Everett; 5913 Woodstock Ct., Virginia Beach, VA 23464

Frick, Paul, Graphic Design; 378 7th St., N.E., Atlanta, GA 30308

Gambetta-Bollmer Graphic Design; 5370 Leaf Back Dr., West Chester, OH 45069

Giarnella Design; 43 Linwood St., New Britain, CT 06052

Graphic Concepts; 4340 Carter Creek Pkwy., Suite 104, Bryan, TX 77801

Graphic & Photo Art; 2650 Mock Orange Dr., Salt Lake City, UT 84119

Harland, John H., Company; PO Box 105250, Atlanta, GA 30348

Heiman, Richard, Advertising, Inc; Tower Place, Penthouse Suite 2950, 3340 Peachtree Road, N.E., Atlanta, GA 30326

Hellman Design Associates, Inc.; PO Box 627, Waterloo, IA 50704

Hill and Knowlton, Inc.; One Illinois Center, 111 E. Wacker Dr., Suite 1700, Chicago, IL 60601

Horwitz, Mann & Bukvic Advertising; 2241 Losantiville Rd., Cincinnati, OH 45237

Hucknall, Nanette; 336-C Adolphus Ave., Cliffside Park, NJ 07010

Ikkanda, Richard, Design Associates; Graphic Design/Advertising, 2800 Twenty-Eighth St., Suite 152, Santa Monica, CA 90405

Image Network, Inc.; 645 West End Ave., 2B, New York, NY 10025

Keating & Associates; Advertising & Public Relations, 2223B Magazine St., New Orleans, LA 70130

Kelly, P.; 3415 Wyandot, Denver, CO 80211

Kinser, Bill, Design; Rd. 1, Boalsburg, PA 16827

Kosterman, Wayne, Associates, Inc.; Suite G, 955 N. Plum Grove Rd., Schaumburg, IL 60195-4757

Kramer, Miller, Lomden, Glassman; Graphic Design, 1528 Waverly St., Philadelphia, PA 19146

Kutchey, Valerie, Design; 702 N. Eutaw St., Baltimore, MD 21201

Landis, John K., Graphic Design; 438 W. Walnut St., Kutztown, PA 19530

Larrabee Design Associates; 940 N. Negley Ave., Pittsburgh, PA 15206

Lead Advertising and Design; 161 E. Chicago St., Elgin, IL 60120

Leigh, David; 1245 Park Ave., New York, NY 10128

Leitstein, Alan, Graphics; 8360 N.W. 21 Ct., Sunrise, FL 33322

Lesniewicz/Navarre; 222 N. Eric St., Toledo, OH 43624

Lienhart, James, Design; 155 N. Harbor Dr., Chicago, IL 60601

Longo, Stephen, & Associates; Graphic & Package Design, Suite 2C Colfax Manor, Roselle Park, NJ 07204

Lun, Andy; Graphic Designer, 270 Clinton Ave., Brooklyn, NY 11205

Lyons, Richard E.; Richard Heiman Advertising, Inc., Tower Place, Penthouse Suite 2950, 3340 Peachtree Road, N.E., Atlanta, GA 30326

Malone Group, The; 1420 Atlantic Bank Tower, Jacksonville, FL 32202

Matteson, Ron R.; 1638 N. Camelia, Tempe, AZ 85281

Mazzama, Maria; 255 Riverwoods Ln., Burnsville, MN 55337

McDonald, Max, Design Office; 5812 Alcove Ave., N. Hollywood, CA 91607

Mielcarek, Vincent J.; 106 Hatfield Place, PO Box R, Staten Island, NY 10302

Nervig, Carole, Graphic Design; 2120 Thirteenth St., Boulder, CO 80302

Neumeier Design Team; 212 High St., Suite 4, Palo Alto, CA 94301

Olson, Patricia; Cats' Pajamas, 344 Ramsey, Saint Paul, MN 55102

Palazzo Design; 1105½ Beach Ave., Bradley Beach, NJ 07720

Parker, David; Graphic Designer, 34-29 97th St., New York, NY 11368

Pavey, Jerry, Design; 14513 Melinda Ln., Rockville, MD 20853

Persechini & Moss; 357 S. Robertson Blvd., Beverly Hills, CA 90211

Pierce, Ron W.; (address unavailable)

PR Associates, Inc.; Advertising & Public Relations, 1799 Akron-Peninsula Rd., Akron, OH 44313

P.R. Design; 5971 Hillrose Dr., San Jose, CA 95123

Probst, Alison & Robert; 106 Hosea Ave., Cincinnati, OH 45220

Pullara, Paul, Graphic Design; 26 Meadow Dr., Little Falls, NJ 07424

Purdue University; Creative Arts No. 1 Bldg., W. Lafayette, IN 47907

Qually & Company, Inc.; Advertising/ Design/Firm, 2238 Central St., Evanston, IL 60201

Rabe, Peter J.; Graphic & Photo Art, 2650 Mock Orange Dr., Salt Lake City, UT 84119

Ramsden, Rosalie, Graphic Design; 7418 Burning Tree Dr., Houston, TX 77036

Runyan, Robert Miles, & Associates; 200 E. Culver Blvd., Playa de Rey, CA 90293

Schenker, Probst & Barensfeld; 2728 Vine St., Cincinnati, OH 45219

Settleducati, Mark; 218 E. 17th St., New York, NY 10003

Sharan, Jerry, Graphics; 44 Berkshire Rd., Sandy Hook, CT 06482

Shore Design; 250 Columbus Ave., Suite 203, San Francisco, CA 94133

Sloman, Gaynelle W.; Advertising & Design, 405 Capitol St., Suite 700, Charleston, WV 25301

Sommese, Lanny, Design; 481 Glenn Rd., State College, PA 16801

Tscherny, George, Inc.; 238 E. 72 St., New York, NY 10021

Vorisek, R. Seth; 151 Garden Ave., Paramus, NJ 07652

WW3/Papagalos Incorporated; 313 E. Thomas Rd., Suite 208, Phoenix, AZ 85012

Weller Institute, The; 2427 Park Oak Dr., Los Angeles, CA 90068

White, Carl; Doremus & Company, 850 N. Church St., Rockford, IL 61103

Yasumura/CYB; 100 Park Ave., New York, NY 10017

Young & Martin, Inc.; Graphic Communications, 550 Pharr Rd., N.E., Suite 835, Atlanta, GA 30305

Zahor Design Inc.; 150 E. 35th St., New York, NY 10016

Zarwell, Bob; The Design Company, 12201 W. Burleigh, Milwaukee, WI 53222